Hermanos de la Luz
Brothers of the Light

Hermanos de la Luz
Brothers of the Light

Ray John de Aragón

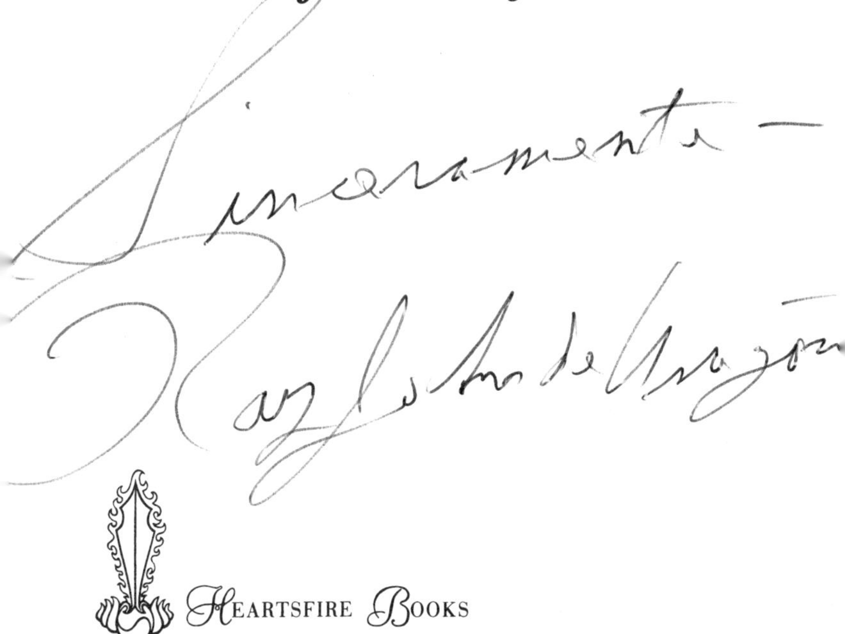

Library of Congress Cataloging-in-Publication Data

De Aragón, Ray John, 1946–

Hermanos de la Luz : Brothers of the Light

Religion/Christianity / Ray John de Aragón.

p. cm.

English and Spanish

ISBN 1-889797-18-9 (cloth) : $16.95

1. Hermanos Penitentes—Prayer-books and devotions— Spanish. 2. Hermanos Penitentes—Prayer-books and devotions—English. 3. Alabados—Texts. 4. New Mexico—Religious life and customs—Sources. I. Title.

BX3653.U6D42 1994 94–17267

242'.802789—dc20 CIP

Cover design by Bill Pfau

Cover art by Ray John de Aragón

Heartsfire Books: 800.988.5170

500 N. Guadalupe Street, Suite G465

Santa Fe, New Mexico 87501 USA

If you are unable to order this book from your local bookseller, you may order directly from the publisher. Quantity discounts for organizations are available.

10 9 8 7 6 5 4 3 2 1

Printed in Canada

Contents

Don Filimón Sánchez, beloved grandfather and member (Hermano Mayor) of the Morada of El Valle de Peñasco Blanco, New Mexico, and Mora, New Mexico.

Preface

Intensive research in the last decades has produced only partial knowledge of the technical, social, artistic, and liturgical aspects of the *Fraternidad Piadosa de los Hermanos de Nuestro Padre Jesús Nazareno* (Pious Fraternity of the Brothers of Our Father Jesus the Nazarene), or *Penitente,* of New Mexico. Surviving traditions and rituals associated with the Penitente have been extensively studied, but a paucity of documentation and conflicting interpretations by scholars have severely limited our understanding of this intensely religious group of men. It remains in dispute, for example, exactly how the Brotherhood began. Contemporary scholars are in general agreement that the Brotherhood is a distinctly New Mexican phenomenon, yet it must not be forgotten that penitential practices were once common in Europe and in other colonies of the New World.

Regardless of their exact origin, the Penitente were true representatives of Spanish religious thought and Spanish culture. The high point of their worship was the re-creation of Christ's Passion on the cross. This was done through portrayal of the suffering of Christ, self-mortification of the flesh, emulation of Christ's Crucifixion, and the singing of *alabados* (sorrowful hymns). Some of the hymns reflect local improvisation. A few undoubtedly originated in sixteenth-century Spain, while others appear to have been written by native poets. The music of the alabados is reminiscent of the Gregorian chants, but with a more primitive strain, like the *saeta* (arrow song) of Seville. The saeta (the word derives from the Latin *sagitta*) is a poetic form that dates back to the sixteenth century. It contains short couplets that are recited to excite religious devotion or penitence during Holy Week processions and church ceremonies. The saeta chants are characteristic of the *cante jondo* (deep song), a very popular type of Spanish song that is often mournful in nature. The rituals and artistic creations of the Penitente aptly expressed their quest for unity with the sufferings of Christ.

My interest in the Penitente has its roots in my early childhood, when my mother and mentor, María Cleofas Sánchez de Aragón, would eagerly relate to me the folklore, legends, traditions, and history of the Hispanics of New Mexico. She was extremely proud of our Spanish heritage, and this pride was reflected in her passing down the folkways and religious customs of *nuestra gente* (our people) to the family.

I wish to thank many for their assistance and their support of this study. First of all, my wife, Rosa María Calles, without whose help and guidance this book never would have gotten done. Others who have offered kind words, advice, and information and have followed the maturation of this work from its initial inception many, many years ago include Máximo de Aragón, my father, whose association and friendship with Miguel Archibeque, Román Aranda, and M. Santos Meléndez, all *Hermano Supremos* (Supreme Brothers) of the Santa Hermandad, provided me with further insights into the Holy Brotherhood; Juan García, my uncle and an *Hermano Mayor* (Elder Brother), who explained the duties of the members to me and taught me how to make a *disciplina* (yucca fibrous whip); Charles Aranda, Román Aranda's son, who happily shared with me, as my friend and supporter, knowledge gained through his father; Horacio Valdéz, *santero* (saint image maker) and member of the Brotherhood, whose friendship and kindness will always be appreciated; Fabiola Cabeza de Baca, who even at an advanced age glowed with happiness while recalling the early days; Fray Angélico Chávez, my friend and well-intentioned critic; and Tibo Chávez, Jesusita Aragón, Sabine Ulibarrí, Eliseo Rodríguez, Gilberto Espinóza, Max Roybal, Pedro Ribera-Ortega, Marc Simmons, Dr. Myra Ellen Jenkins, Marta Weigle, Edwin Berry, Father Thomas Steele, Lorin W. Brown (Lorenzo de Córdova), Padre Benedicto Cuesta, Dr. José R. López Gastón, Dr. Wallace Johnson, Dr. E. Boyd, and Concha Ortíz y Píno de Kleven, each of whose visions and thoughts served to enrich this work. With faith and good hope, I humbly dedicate this work to my grandfather, Filimón Sánchez, born July 17, 1874, Peñasco Blanco, New Mexico, died September 2, 1955, a dedicated member as an *Hermano Mayor* and *Hermano de la Luz* (Brother of Light) of La Fraternidad Piadosa de los Hermanos de Nuestro Padre Jesús Nazareno; and to my grandmother, María Pablita Roméro, born June 25, 1882, Cebolla (LeDoux), New Mexico, died February 2, 1956, a devoted member of the lay women's order of *Las Carmelitas* (*Las Hermanas de Nuestra Señora del Carmen*).

I

Historical Background

Engraving from La Imitación de Cristo *(The Imitation of Christ) by St. Thomas á Kempis (1380?–1471).*

Origin of the Penitente Brotherhood

The Fraternidad Piadosa de los Hermanos de Nuestro Padre Jesús Nazareno is a confraternity of Spanish-American men from the area of Tomé, south of Albuquerque, from northern New Mexico, and from southern Colorado. It is dedicated to the provision of mutual aid and community charity, the spirit of penance, and the Passion of Jesus Christ.[1] Vestiges of this group exist today, but the rigorous devotion of centuries past is no longer widespread. The Penitentes formerly consecrated themselves to the Passion of Christ in remembrance of the fact that he was condemned, was crucified, and died on the cross for the expiation of the sins of mankind.[2] Each year during Lent the Penitentes reenacted the Passion of the Savior through the use of polychrome religious art, religious ballads, and personal atonement.[3]

The self-flagellation performed by New Mexico's Penitentes is a continuation of certain religious practices prevalent in Spain during the Middle Ages. These practices, in fact, had their origins in early Christian history. In the first century, the Passion of Christ began to receive special attention. The church had its center in the Holy Land, where relics of the Passion were the objects of intense veneration and devotion. According to biblical scripture, Jesus Christ had left a

Nuestra Señora de la Soledad y el Ecce Homo *(Our Lady of Solitude and the Man of Sorrows). Courtesy Museum of New Mexico, neg. no. 129519.*

request on the night before he was crucified: "Do this and remember me." This statement may have been interpreted throughout different periods of history as an injunction to mortify the flesh in the reenactment of the Passion.

For the two thousand years between the time of Moses and the time of Jesus, the Jews had commemorated the Passover, their freedom from slavery and persecution in Egypt. Each year the Jewish people would gather to recount what had happened. In this way, they were able to keep alive the memory of the persecution and religious beliefs of their ancestors. The retelling of the story and the reenactment of the events kept their religion going and pulled the people together. Similarly, the first Christians commemorated the Passion of Jesus Christ.

Mary, the mother of Christ, it is written, reenacted the Passion—from the washing of the feet to the Crucifixion—as a remembrance and a penance. She also visited each place of the Passion. Mary was taken to Ephesus by the Apostle John, the youngest of the apostles and the cousin of Jesus, to escape religious persecution. St. James, the brother of John, on occasion shared the same home at Ephesus. It was St. James who traveled to Spain to publicize the story of Jesus. He succeeded in spreading the faith throughout Spain, and he and his followers built the first chapel in honor of Mary, which still remains standing. After many years, St. James returned from Spain to his homeland, where he was beheaded by Herod. His relics were taken to Spain, and he was recognized as the patron of the country and buried at Santiago de Compostella, the site of the chapel he had built.

St. Ignatius of Antioch,[4] a disciple of St. John (the apostle who remained with Mary until she died), nurtured the devotion of the Passion by writing, "Him I seek who died on our behalf, Him I desire who rose again for our sake. Permit me to be an imitator of the Passion of my God."[5] Other ascetic imitators of the Passion included the Origenists, followers of Origen, one of the first interpreters of scripture in the late second century and early third century, and the *apostolici*. Both of these groups devoted themselves to lives of penance and prayer. Apostolici was a term applied at various periods to "reformers wishing to return to the primitive Church, poor, humble, simple and penitential, through close imitation of the Apostles. Some Gnostic communities in Asia Minor from the second to the fourth centuries were called 'apostolici' by Epiphanius."[6] St. Epiphanius of Cyprus (315–402), a Church Father, lived during the primary period of the apostolici.

During the early persecution of the Christians by the Romans, some ascetics took refuge in the Egyptian desert. One of these was St. Anthony of Egypt, born in upper Egypt about the middle of the third century and considered the father of monasticism. Although there were many hermits before him, it was St. Anthony who organized the hermits into associations and fostered their adherence to the principles of chastity, poverty, labor, and mortification of the flesh. St. Anthony's austere way of living spread throughout the civilized world, and soon there were monasteries everywhere.

Because of internal changes within the Roman Empire, Christianity was eventually accepted, and the persecution of Christians came to an end. During this same period, the ecclesiastical church became better organized, and by the end of the fourth century monks began attacking heresy, crime, and religious abuse perpetrated by bishops and priests. One of these monks was St. Jerome (340–420). St. Jerome lived for four years in the Syrian desert, where he devoted himself to the practice of penance and the study of Hebrew and the Scriptures.

The monastic system declined by the end of the fifth century but was revived by St. Benedict (480–543), the father of Western monasticism. At the age of seventeen, St. Benedict fled his life of leisure to live in a cave for three years as a hermit. He soon had many followers, and they formed a community of individuals who, like St. Benedict, participated in the Lord's Passion.

St. Benedict's followers became the pioneers of Christian civilization. These monks and devout women began to live under the protection of the church and provided social services and religious instruction. The monks preached the Gospel, cared for the poor and sick, taught religion to the young, cleared forests, laid roads, built bridges, and cultivated barren lands. In the sixth, seventh, and eighth centuries, monasticism became more and more widespread, and many priests became monks and followed the rules laid down by St. Benedict.

In the tenth century, important reforms were inaugurated at Cluny, a town in east-central France. These reforms reshaped Benedictine life, and during the eleventh century, many Benedictines left their monasteries to become priests and to serve communities neglected because of the lack of secular clergy. St. Peter Damian (1007–1072), a strong supporter of the Cluniac reforms, introduced the use of a whip with cords for self-flagellation and encouraged other monasteries, including Monte Cassino, to adopt the practice of self-flagellation.[7] St. Damian was also one of the first to voice the ideal of apostolic poverty that spread in the following century and culminated in the mendicant orders.[8]

In 1098, a new monastery was established at Citeaux. Originally very strict, discipline at the monastery became lax, and scandalous behavior was rampant. As a consequence, St. Bernard (1090–1153) entered the monastery with twenty-seven lay brothers and remained there for three years to restore the rule of St. Benedict.

The eloquent appeals of St. Bernard in favor of the religious life helped increase the number of those seeking a religious vocation.[9] He was called the "oracle" of the twelfth century and founded 168 monasteries. Furthermore, besides advocating the original vows of chastity, poverty, labor, and mortification of the flesh, St. Bernard also promoted the Charter of Charity, sometimes referred to as the "Cistercian Magna Carta." His defense of the Cistercian charter was so ardent that the Benedictines at Cluny and eventually all other monasteries adopted the Cistercian rule. The charter increased religious fervor and caused tens of thousands to devote themselves to prayer and the practice of austerities.

Christians under the guidance of apostolici utilized the tragic drama of the Passion of Christ along with flagellation as a means of purification and atonement. But excessive self-punishment slowly crept into the rituals.

In medieval days penance took forms other than the self-applied whip. Sometimes it was as severe as willing crucifixion in reenactment of the death of Jesus Christ; sometimes a long, arduous pilgrimage; sometimes the amputation of an offending limb or organ; sometimes a withdrawal from all human social contacts; sometimes, even, an eager walk directly into the unexplored realm of death itself.

But the flagellanti, as a religious expression in a comprehensive society, rose as a sect, or movement, early in the eleventh century, half a century or so before the birth of St. Francis. Until that time, extreme physical penance was a frequent and well-known human phenomen, but was quite unorganized.[10]

In the twelfth century, heretics were dealt with severely. At first ecclesiastical authorities reproved civil rules for their cruelty, but later the church sanctioned repressive measures against flagellants, many of whom were burned at the stake. St. Bernard, among others, vigorously protested the use of violence against flagellants and even wrote a defense of his flagellant followers.

Itinerant barefoot preachers and religious hermits continued to use flagellation as a form of penance. Their loyalty to the doctrine of the church was never questioned, but their methods of expressing their faith were strongly criticized and they were eventually persecuted.[11]

St. Francis of Assisi (1182–1226), one of the most beloved saints, exhibited a religious zeal of unmatched profundity. After converting to Catholicism, he renounced wealth and embraced poverty, sought to imitate Christ, and became especially devoted to the Mother of Jesus.[12] He also introduced a new element into the celebration of the Passion: the use of crucifixes, which provided a representation of the human Christ as an aid for those intent upon sharing Christ's suffering.

The Franciscan Order, founded by St. Francis, became one of the most powerful of the monastic orders and was subdivided into three major divisions. The First Order, founded in

San Francisco de Asís *(St. Francis of Assisi). Eighteenth-century engraving, Mexico. De Aragón family collection.*

1209, consisted of ordained priests and lay brothers. The Second Order, founded in 1212, consisted of contemplative nuns. The Third Order, founded in 1219 under the name of the Brothers and Sisters of Penance, was a lay order of men and women living in society. All other tertiaries (including members of the Third Order of St. Dominic, founded in 1286) and the Carmelite Sisters (an amalgamation of different women's orders) used the rule of St. Francis.[13]

The Third Order of Penance was inspired by humanitarian ideals and followed the rules of St. Francis, who also adopted the charter promoted by St. Bernard as set forth by Cardinal Hugolino (later Pope Gregory IX):

> It provides that brethren and sisters of penitence living in their own houses should dress plainly, eat and drink with moderation, avoid dances and plays, keep certain fasts, observe the canonical hours at home or in church, confess thrice a year, pay their debts and restore any goods which belonged to others, live peaceably, not bear arms, abstain from oaths, contribute to the support of poor or sick members and others, and attend the funerals of deceased members. . . . New members were admitted by the ministers, with the approval of some discreet brethren, after promising to observe the conditions and after a year's probation; once admitted, no one might withdraw from the fraternity except to join a religious Order. . . . The fraternity met once a month in a church selected by the ministers, and should on these occasions, if it was convenient, be instructed by a religious.[14]

The Franciscan missionaries quickly spread into numerous European countries, including France, Spain, and England. They adopted the "discipline of rule"—the custom of self-flagellation common to all medieval religious orders.[15] Under church supervision, self-flagellation was prescribed, regulated, and encouraged during Lent and on other designated days.

The issue of absolute poverty divided the Franciscans into two factions. One faction advocated following the original rule of St. Francis while the other favored the acquisition of property and material goods to support members of the order. St. Bonaventure (1221–1274), biographer of St. Francis and founder of the Franciscan school of theology, was called upon to settle the dispute. The division continued, however, despite the fact that the church hierarchy favored the relaxed viewpoint and ultimately condemned the so-called Spirituals. After the church imprisoned or burned some of the Spirituals as heretics, many of those remaining became associated with the Fraticelli, which were flagellant brotherhoods and processions composed of lay men and women as well as clergy.

The Black Death and the Italian earthquakes of 1348, together with the spiritual shock caused by conflict between and within church and state, helped revive the popularity of flagellation as a form of penance. Jean de Venette, a Carmelite friar and master of theology at the University of Paris, described the processions of the flagellants that occurred in response to the plague:

> While the plague was still active and spreading from town to town, men in Germany, Flanders, Hainault and Lorraine uprose and began a new sect on their own authority. Stripped to the waist, they gathered in large groups and bands and marched in procession through the crossroads and squares of cities and good towns. They formed circles and beat upon their backs with weighted scourges, rejoicing as

they did so in loud voices and singing hymns suitable to their rite and newly composed for it. Thus, for 33 days they marched through many towns doing penance and affording a great spectacle to the wondering people. They flogged their shoulders and arms, scourged with iron points so zealously as to draw blood.[16]

Jean Froissart gave this account:

The penitents went about, coming first out of Germany. They were men who did public penance and scourged themselves with whips of hard knotted leather with little iron spikes. Some made themselves bleed very badly between the shoulder blades and some foolish women had cloths ready to catch the blood and smear it on their eyes, saying it was miraculous blood. While they were doing penance, they sang very mournful songs about nativity and the passion of our Lord. The object of this penance was to put a stop to the mortality, for in that time . . . at least a third of all the people in the world died.[17]

The chronicler Henry of Hereford sketched a depiction similar to the portrayals of the Penitentes of New Mexico in the nineteenth century. He described the flagellants as:

. . . proceeding with hymns to a church, where they would disrobe except for a waistcloth and flagellate themselves. Then they would lie on the ground outside the church in various postures, symbolizing their sins, and ask God's pardon. They resumed their procession and singing, and each time they came to a verse mentioning Christ's passion they would fall to the ground, regardless of mud, thistles, or stones.[18]

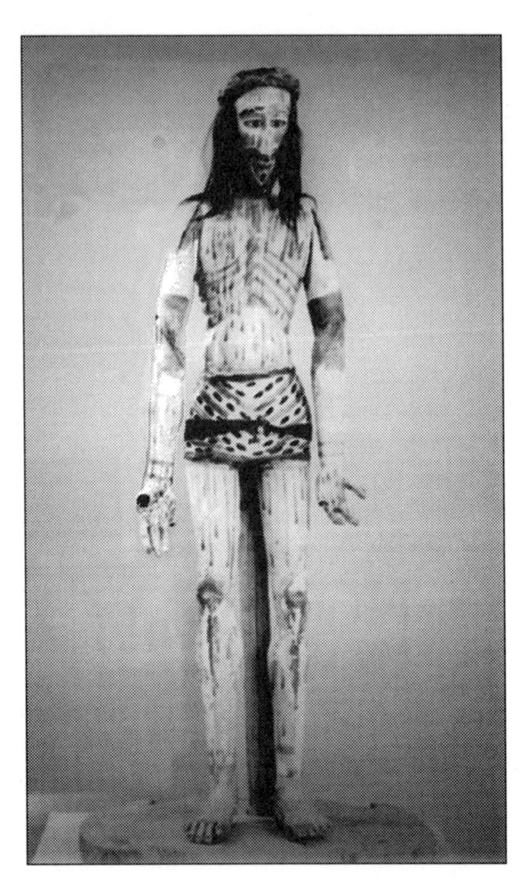

Nuestro Padre Jesús Nazareno *(Our Father Jesus of Nazareth). Nineteenth-century, New Mexico. Courtesy Museum of New Mexico, neg. no. 59415.*

At the request of the University of Paris, Pope Clement VI condemned the flagellants in 1349, sending his decree to all the bishops of France, Germany, Poland, and England. A few of the flagellant groups defied the church. These groups developed into organized religious sects with their own ceremonies and heretical doctrines. According to Robert B. McCoy,

> The flagellanti became heretics and most heretical of these was the Bianchi of Italy and a group led by Karl Schmidt of Thuringia.

Both the Bianchi and followers of Schmidt adopted habits and rules similar to those of the Franciscan orders, and both groups defied the jurisdiction and authority of the Holy Church. At the same time, both proclaimed devotion to God and the teaching of the Catholic faith. The situation could be resolved only by the church suppressing the heresy—Schmidt and the leaders of the Bianchi were captured and burned at the stake.[19]

A group of women flagellants known as the Beguines arose during the high Middle Ages, and they shared similarities with the Apostolici, Fraticelli, and Franciscan Spirituals. The Carmelite Sisters derived from the Beguines and were especially prevalent in Spain, where they had originated.

Clerical misconduct was rampant during the fourteenth century, and the poor were unable to protect themselves from injustice. The monks were on the side of the people, and as a result the conflict between them and the secular clergy increased. In the period 1378–1417, a schism occurred, and three popes laid claim to the Holy See.

St. Vincent Ferrer, a Dominican preacher born January 23, 1350, in Valencia, Spain, arose as a champion of the poor and the oppressed,[20] and he was asked by ecclesiastical leaders to settle the dispute within the church. Along with St. Colette (1381–1447), a member of the Poor Clare's (Second Franciscan Order), and others, St. Vincent arranged for a new election, which resulted in the selection of Cardinal Colonne, who took the name Pope Martin V. St. Vincent acquired an army of penitent flagellant followers while traveling into the plague-stricken areas of Europe. He often led processions consisting of thousands of penitents in Spain, Switzerland, France, Italy, England, Ireland, and Scotland.

The Council of Constance (1414–1418) condemned the flagellant movement, and the Disciplinati were again forced underground. The practice of flagellation gradually subsided, but in the sixteenth century the Jesuits revived lay interest in self-inflicted flagellation, especially in the southern European countries. St. Ignatius of Loyola (1491–1556), founder of the Jesuits in Spain, stressed the Passion as a means of supporting virtue and enduring affliction.

St. Ignatius was reared in the court of Ferdinand V of Aragón and Isabella of Castile.[21] These two monarchs financed the voyage of Christopher Columbus (who was a member of the Third Order of St. Francis). By 1511, Franciscans had already established a monastery and a school for boys on the island of Hispaniola, where Columbus had landed in 1493.[22]

After the conquest of Mexico by Hernán Cortés in 1521, Mexico was quickly evangelized by the Franciscans. The friars championed the cause of the Native Americans in the New World from the time of their arrival. By the middle of the century, there were eighty Franciscan monasteries and nearly four hundred missionaries in New Spain. Missionary colleges were established at Queretaro (1531) and Zacatecas (1546), and the University of Mexico was opened in 1553. The University received the same academic privileges as the University of Salamanca and possessed chairs of theology, scripture, canon law, civil law, arts, rhetoric, grammar, and medicine.[23] Franciscan friars were sent into northern Mexico and New Mexico by the late sixteenth century.

Penitential activities were introduced into New Mexico with the arrival of Don Juan de Oñate and his colonists in 1598. Under the spiritual guidance of Franciscan friars, the colonists observed Holy Week on the bank of a small stream. The Lenten observance was chronicled by the group's historian, Gaspar Pérez de Villagra, in his epic poem *Historia de la Nueva México:*

> The army again broke camp and we journeyed onward until we reached the banks of another stream. The friars named this river the Sacramento for the reason that we arrived at its banks on Holy Thursday, the feast of the Blessed Sacrament. In order to observe properly this most holy day, Don Juan ordered a large chapel built. In the center we placed a representation of the Holy Sepulcher. A special guard of honor stood watch the entire day and night. Here in the evening the priest and all the officers and men came and devoutly, on their knees, with tears in their eyes, begged forgiveness for their sins. They prayed to Our Blessed Lord, that He, who walked with safety upon the waters, He who led the children of Israel through the trackless deserts, would have mercy and compassion on them and lead them safely through the arid places through which they wandered. They asked Him to guard over them and aid them to carry His Holy Faith to the remote regions of New Mexico.

The night was one of prayer and penance for all. The women and children came barefoot to pray at the holy shrine. The soldiers, with cruel scourges, beat their backs unmercifully until the camp ran crimson with their blood. The humble Franciscan friars, barefoot and clothed in cruel thorny girdles, devoutly chanted their doleful hymns, praying forgiveness for their sins.

Don Juan, unknown to anyone except me, went to a secluded spot where he cruelly scourged himself, mingling bitter tears with the blood which flowed from his many wounds. This continued throughout the camp till early morn. . . . Geronimo and I took example from these worthy ones and underwent like punishment. What lessons we learned from what we observed that day![24]

In the seventeenth century, Spain suffered political and spiritual decline. Under Philip IV (1621–1665), the empire began to crumble, although New Spain prospered and a church hierarchy was solidly in place. A diocese was established in Durango in 1620, the same year that the Pilgrims landed at Plymouth Rock. The church hierarchy in Mexico included 6 archbishops and 30 bishops, nearly all of Spanish birth. In the Spanish colonies during the first century and a half, all but 12 of the 369 bishops were born in Spain.[25]

In 1630, Fray Alonso de Benavidez made mention of the custom of flagellation in New Mexico in a report addressed to King Philip IV of Spain:

I cannot refrain from telling here a saying of the Demon, by the mouth in an Indian Wizard who was convinced of the word of God, when I began the conversion of the great pueblo of the Xumanas, the which I dedicated to the glorious San Isidoro, Archbishop of Sevilla, because of having begun the conversion on his day.

And it befell that seeing himself convinced, and that under my reasoning all the pueblo had determined to be Christian, the Wizard was much angered and said at the top of his voice: "You Spaniards and Christians, how crazy you are! And you live like crazy folks! You want to teach us that we be crazy also!" I asked him wherein we were crazy. And he must have seen some procession of penance during Holy Week in some pueblo of Christians and so he said: "You Christians are so crazy people in the streets shedding your blood. And thus you must wish that this pueblo be also crazy!" And with this, greatly angered and yelling [*dando voces*] he went forth from the pueblo, saying that he did not wish to be crazy. Over which matter we were left laughing, and I much more, since I recognized and was persuaded that it was the Demon, who thus went fleeing confounded by the virtue of the Divine Word.[26]

In 1680, increasing discontentment among the Indians of New Mexico over their maltreatment by the Spaniards culminated in the Great Pueblo Rebellion. The Spaniards were also blamed for a severe drought, which the Indians were certain was caused by the introduction of the Christian religion. There were more than fifty friars and fifty-thousand converts in the pueblo villages surrounding Santa Fe at the time of the revolt. Popé, one of the most masterful Indian leaders of all time, united the Pueblo people. He was born and raised at San Juan Pueblo but moved to Taos, the northernmost of the pueblos, where he established his base of operations. The Indians rebelled en masse, destroying the churches and ranches; killing men, women, and children; and burning their sacred images. A small group of Spaniards survived and made their way out of the territory to El Paso del Norte, taking with them the polychrome image of *Nuestra Senora del Rosario* (Our Lady of the Rosary, popularly known as Our Lady of the Conquest).

At the time of the revolt, the number of Indians living in the Rio Grande Valley was approximately thirty thousand. The number of Spanish colonists was approximately twenty-five hundred. When the survivors were finally assembled near El Pasodel Norte, the governor was able to list only 1,936, and this number included 317 Indians who had fought on their side.[27]

During the twelve years that followed (1680–1692), the Pueblo Indians realized the dream of all oppressed people by becoming masters of their own territory once again and returning to their old ways. Popé and his followers set out to remove all signs of the Spanish, beginning with the churches. Church records were burned, as were the crosses in the cemeteries. The Indians who had converted to Catholicism had to wash off the effects of baptism in the river.

The Spanish had introduced many good things into New Mexico: sheep, cattle, wheat and other grains, fruit trees, and tools and utensils of many different types. Although all these things had substantially raised the Indians' standard of living, Popé directed that these improvements had to go. One Spanish innovation, however, was adopted by Popé: the requirement that the Indians pay taxes in the form of food, blankets, and other supplies. Popé and his men did the collecting this time instead of the Spanish.[28]

Popé's dream turned into a nightmare. The drought persisted, the harvests were meager, and the Apaches and Navajos raided and looted the pueblos. More than eight pueblos were destroyed by these raiders, and one whole

Morada altar, Taos, New Mexico. Courtesy Kit Carson Museum Foundation.

San Francisco de Asís *(St. Francis of Assisi). Polychromed wood sculpture and nicho, by Ray John de Aragón.*

Pueblo group, the Piros of southern New Mexico, was wiped out. Some of the pueblos made war on each other, an activity never permitted under the Spanish. The Tanos, after being driven out of their pueblos, settled in Santa Fe and surrounding areas. Popé lost his power over the Indians after five years and was replaced in 1685 by his lieutenant, Tupatu. He regained his position in 1688 but died a year later, when Tupatu once again took his place. "The Indians of New Mexico made the sad discovery that while living with and under the Spanish was an extremely difficult proposition, living without them was even worse."[29]

In the meantime, the viceroy and his officials in New Spain had appointed Don Diego de Vargas Zapata Luján Ponce de León (1643–1704) as the governor of New Mexico, which was not considered much of a prize because of its vastness, its poverty, and its distance from the main population centers in Mexico. The Franciscans had never been able to maintain a proper quota of clergy, and communication had always been a problem.

Don Diego de Vargas, born in Madrid to a noble family, had gone to the New World looking for adventure. He was deeply religious, and he provided hope and enthusiasm to the discouraged and dispirited New Mexican colony in exile. He spent a large sum of his own money in the reconquest of the northern lands and received little in return except for a secure place in the chronicles of the region. During their return journey, the colonists found all the pueblos deserted. Many had been permanently abandoned because of the Apache raids. The colonists continued up the Rio Grande Valley expecting to engage in battle at Santa Fe. On September 13, 1692, they appeared before the walls of that pueblo, catching the Tanos by surprise. There was no battle. The following morning, De Vargas promised that the Spanish would take no revenge for the revolt of twelve years earlier and that no harm would come to the Indians if they would accept Spanish rule. The Tanos consented to this condition, and De Vargas and three Franciscan priests who had accompanied him entered the pueblo unarmed. In the next few days, many of the Indian leaders from the north appeared in Santa Fe to make peace. At San Juan Pueblo, De Vargas met with Tupatu, who requested help in resisting the Apache attacks, which were seriously hurting the pueblos.

After the reconquest of New Mexico, the former confraternities were reestablished. These included the Third Order of St. Francis, which, according to a report sent by Fray Cayetano José Bernal to Governor Fernando Chacón in October 1794, was reinstituted in 1692, and the confraternity of Our Lady of Carmel, which was licensed in 1710.[30]

Some of the older settlements were rebuilt, and new ones were established. Supplies were slow in coming from New Spain and sometimes failed to arrive. The New Mexican colonists basically had to depend on themselves. Indeed, in the case of religion, because the friars worked in the pueblos, the colonists were sometimes spiritually neglected. The confraternities, under the guidance of the friars, helped solidify the relationship between the scattered Spanish settlements and the church.

Spain was gradually transformed during the eighteenth century. By the end of the century, the old Catholic aristocracy of Spain had ceased to exist. Spain's hold over the colonies grew less and less secure. Finally, in 1808, Spain abandoned the church. Church property was confiscated, and monasteries were suppressed. But the Old World ways were now deeply entrenched in New Mexico and the rest of the Southwest. In California, twenty-one missions prospered under the direction of Junipero Serra, a Franciscan friar. The Franciscans also established many missions in Arizona.

The relationship between the Old World flagellant brotherhoods and the penitential practices of the Third Order of St. Francis in New Mexico is clearly discernible. In 1775, Fray Francisco Atanasio Domínguez, who was appointed canonical visitor to New Mexico, was ordered to submit a report on the status of the church. He discovered that Franciscans and members of the Third Order of St. Francis were involved in penitential activities, including self-flagellation during Holy Week.[31] In 1776, he documented the performance of a Passion Play in Tomé, New Mexico, a Penitente stronghold, that included self-flagellation.[32] Fray Domínguez also referred to Lenten "exercises" of the Third Order of St. Francis under the supervision of the priest at Santa Cruz (also called Santa Cruz de la Cañada) for "feasts of Our Lady, rosary with the father in church, Fridays of Lent, *Via Crucis* with the father, and later, after dark, discipline attended by those who came voluntarily."[33] The same report included an inventory of the transept altar of the chapel of the Third Order that was part of the Santa Cruz church. Listed were an image of St. Francis on a litter, a statue of *Jesús Nazareno*[34] (Jesus of Nazareth), a statue of *Nuestra Señora de los Dolores*[35] (Our Lady of Sorrows), a bench, and a wooden cross.[36]

Bishop Don Pedro Tamarón y Romeral, of the diocese of Durango, began to recall Franciscan missionaries from New Mexico as early as 1760. The Spanish Franciscan clergy in

La Santísima Trinidad *(The Holy Trinity). Nineteenth-century, New Mexico. De Aragón family collection.*

San Francisco de Asís *(St. Francis of Assisi). Nineteenth-century, New Mexico. De Aragón family collection.*

Mexico had begun to dwindle in number as a result of a revolutionary movement directed against Spain. One consequence was that the spiritual needs of New Mexicans were neglected. Bishop Tamarón believed the missions of New Mexico would be better served by secular priests, but these priests were met with open opposition by the people. The large isolated region of New Mexico was left with only a handful of Franciscan clergy.

The recall of the Franciscans was never complete. A few of the friars continued to hold on to their old posts and were oblivious of the sweeping changes in religious thought that were occurring. In their isolation, some of the Franciscans continued to foster Old World interpretations of religious observances. This was also the case in other parts of New Spain. The secular priests tried to change this, and the Third Order of St. Francis steadily withdrew underground.[37] The closeness of the relationship between the New Mexican colonists and the Franciscans was summarized by Pedro Bautista Pino in an exposition sent to the Spanish Crown in 1812: "As the religion of St. Francis was that of the conquest and had remained the only one, New Mexicans were so accustomed to seeing their habit that they would hardly accept any other. Therefore, the first religious and bishop would have to be Franciscans."[38]

In 1817, Bishop Juan Francisco Márquez de Castañiza sent Juan Bautista Ladrón del Niño de Guevara on an ecclesiastical visit to New Mexico. In his investigation of the churches and chapels of the territory, de Guevara found a chapel used by the Third Order in Santa Fe with human skulls on its altar. De Guevara rebuked the Third Order Brothers for their use of exposed human skulls and ordered the chapel demolished.[39] De Guevara remained in New Mexico until 1820 to ascertain that these types of chapels did not exist. He therefore inadvertently forced the Third Order further underground. The Brothers, in fact, constructed separate places of worship called *moradas* (*morada* is derived from the word *morar*, which means to inhabit or reside in a place).

In 1826, Don Agustín Fernández de San Vicente, the second visitor general, reported there were only nine Franciscans and five secular priests ministering in New Mexico. At this time *Presbítero* (Father) Don Antonio José Martínez, a native secular priest born in Abiquiú in 1793, was appointed delegate minister of the Third Order of St. Francis.[40]

Because of the political unrest in the fledgling republic, the withdrawal of the Franciscan clergy, and the distrust felt by the New Mexicans toward the new secular clergy sent from Mexico, Antonio José Martínez made a decision to come to the aid of his people. On March 10, 1817, at the age of twenty-four, he entered the Tridentine Seminary of Durango to begin his studies for the priesthood and was ordained as a secular priest five years later.

Presbítero Don Antonio José Martínez returned to New Mexico as the first native-born secular priest. Although Franciscan and secular ideology were not compatible, Martínez, whose philosophy had been molded by the Franciscans, followed the example of his mentors. Indeed, he was not unlike the many monks who became priests in previous generations and served districts whose religious needs had been neglected by the lack of local clergy.

El Supremo (the Supreme One) or *El Conciliador* (the Conciliator), as Padre Martínez was called by the Penitentes, set the example for the strongly religious people of New

Mexico. The Penitentes carried out many religious functions themselves because of the scarcity of priests, and they and the Carmelitas, influenced by the padre's dedication to works of mercy and virtue, actually aided the clergy in the preservation of the Catholic faith.

In April 1831, a group of sixty Brothers of the Third Order from Santa Cruz de la Cañada submitted a letter of request to Vícar Juan Rafael Rascón. They asked for permission to hold their Lenten exercises in Taos, the area supervised by Padre Martínez. Approval was granted with the stipulation that penitential observances should be performed with moderation.[41]

Also in 1831, Josiah Gregg, an American merchant, was present at a Passion Play performed at Tomé similar to the play described by Fray Domínguez in 1776:

> I once chanced to be in the town of Tomé on Good Friday, when my attention was arrested by a man almost naked, bearing, in imitation of Simon, a huge cross upon his shoulders, which, though constructed of the lightest wood, must have weighed over a hundred pounds. The long end dragged upon the ground, as we have seen it represented in sacred pictures, and about the middle swung a stone of immense dimensions, appended there for the purpose of making the task more laborious.[42]

In 1833, however, José Antonio Laureano de Zubiría y Escalante, Bishop of Durango, visited New Mexico and issued a decree condemning the Brothers of the Third Order for their penitential activities:

> There is, beyond a doubt, a Brotherhood of Penitentes at Santa Cruz de la Cañada which had already been in existence for a number of

years, without authorization or knowledge of the bishops, who certainly would not have given their consent to such a Brotherhood, even if it had been asked. The very open, excessive corporal penances which they are accustomed to practice on certain days of the year, even publicly, are quite contrary to the Church. Among other things or improprieties which it is possible to bring up, there is nothing which conforms to Christian humility.

In order that such practices not be allowed to remain unmanageable, even the construction of a room intended for the housing of instruments of mortification or meeting of Penitentes, if they should ask, may not be permitted by any priest. If they sometimes flagellate themselves with due moderation, they have a place of worship in which they can congregate. Since it is necessary to put an end to the abuses of this kind, which will sometime bring grief to the Holy Church, trusting the conscience of our parochial priests in this *villa,* both present and future, we strictly command that in the future they not permit such meeting of Penitentes for any reason. The room in which they have kept their crosses, etc., if not the property of a definite individual, may remain in the service of the Holy Parochial Church. The aforesaid instruments must be destroyed, although each one may take his own to his house, without its ever again being used by a congregation or Brothers of such a Brotherhood of Penance, which we annul and which must remain no longer active. All are ordered to strict obedience in this rule of the Prelate, penance being one of the most acceptable sacrifices which can be made in the eyes of God.

And we furthermore decree with equal strictness that if the priest of this parish comes to understand that there are any other such meetings of Brotherhoods of Penitentes in parishes of this territory, in order to prevent them, he must advise the appropriate priest, mentioning this Decree, for we do not wish other similar abuse in any area of this Territory.

> Moderate penance, which is beneficial to the spirit, is not prohibited; but totally illegal gatherings incorrectly called Brotherhoods are. Each one who is of good faith and desires self-penance, not destruction, must take up the usual instruments, but they must take them up in private.[43]

During his visit, Zubiría commended Martínez for his humanitarian concerns. The bishop was well aware of Martínez's stand on obligatory tithing. In 1830, anticlericals confiscated church finances and ecclesiastical properties, and the Mexican Church then began to follow a policy of obligatory tithing. Tithes during the Spanish period in New Mexico were paid mostly by providing agricultural produce. Padre Martínez fought against tithing by writing expositions in opposition to it. Despite the fact that free speech was prohibited by the government, some of the Mexican clergy began to reprint and circulate his expositions. The padre gained support from the church, and after four years, at risk of persecution, he was able to get a policy of voluntary offerings substituted for the mandatory policy.

Bishop Zubiría empowered Padre Martínez to administer the sacraments, which were usually performed only by bishops, through the special indulgence of Pope Gregory XVI. Realizing there was a need for more religious and educational leaders in New Mexico, the padre requested permission to establish a seminary in Taos. Bishop Zubiría consented. The seminary became an extension of the coeducational schools Padre Martínez founded in November 1826 at Ranchos de Taos. Padre Martínez also purchased his own printing press and was able to distribute printed materials throughout the territory.

During the year of Zubiría's visit, Antonio Barreiro, a legal adviser in New Mexico, gave this account of religious affairs in the territory:

Spiritual administration in New Mexico is in a truly doleful condition. Nothing is more common than to see an infinite number of the sick die without confession or extreme unction. It is indeed unusual to see the Eucharist administered to the sick. Corpses remain unburied for many days, and children are baptized at the cost of a thousand hardships. A great many unfortunate people spend most of the Sundays of the year without hearing mass. Churches are in a state of near ruin, and most of them are unworthy of being called the temple of God.[44]

Because of these conditions, members of the Brotherhood adhered to traditional benevolent practices and to their devotional forms of penance. These forms of penance were legitimate extensions of the old Franciscan Lenten observances. In 1845, Bishop Zubiría returned to New Mexico and found the Penitentes more active than ever. The bishop ordered a second reading of his decree of 1833, admonishing the Penitentes to engage in more moderate penitential practices. Zubiría's mandate was ineffective in stopping the excesses, but it did force the Penitentes to become highly secretive. They performed their acts of penance in their moradas, which became more prevalent as the pressure from Bishop Zubiría and his aides increased.

During the mid 1830s, Padre Martínez began publishing *El Crepusculo* (The Dawn), a local newspaper. *El Crepusculo* was intended to signal the twilight of one era and the dawn of a new era for New Mexico. Padre Martínez also defended the Penitente Brotherhood by publishing a tract

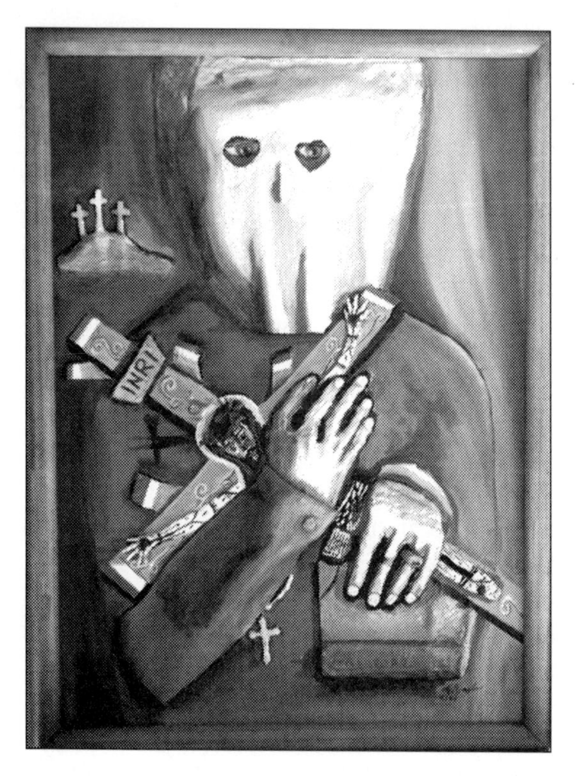

Alabado—*Bas relief; acrylic on canvas with inlayed turquoise, wood, and leather, by Ray John de Aragón.*

entitled *El Instituto Religioso de la Santa Hermandad* (The Religious Institution of the Holy Brotherhood). This tract, which is no longer extant, was written shortly after Zubiría criticized the group for their penitential excesses, including self- flagellation.

In 1846, New Mexico became a territory of the United States. It was still, however, a medieval enclave in the New World, preserving Old World traditions and language. The incoming Americans, who were perceived by the New Mexicans as intruders, viewed New Mexico as a conquered territory, which provided them with an excuse to disregard the native cultural heritage, customs, and history.

In 1851, Jean Baptiste Lamy, appointed the first American bishop of New Mexico, arrived in the territory. A native Frenchman, he experienced cultural shock when he encountered not only English-speaking Americans but also Spanish-speaking natives and a heavy concentration of American Indians who were already converted Catholics. Lamy later tried to create a little France in New Mexico by introducing French architecture and by replacing the native clergy with his own countrymen. He also was led to condemn the Penitentes and eventually their spiritual leader, Padre Antonio José Martínez. Bishop Lamy's attitudes and personal convictions, like those of many of the Americans who came to New Mexico, were set long before his arrival. As shown in this quotation written after many, many years in New Mexico, he was unable to relate to the culture of the native New Mexicans:

Our Mexican population has quite a sad future. Very few of them will be able to follow modern progress. They cannot be compared to the Americans in the way of intellectual liveliness, ordinary skills, and industry; they will thus be scorned and considered an inferior race. . . . The morals, manners, and customs of our unfortunate people are quite different from those of the Americans. With the best possible intentions, those who would not try to understand our worshippers or would not become interested in their well-being, would have trouble in adapting to their spirit, which is almost too primitive.[45]

But Catholicism in New Mexico not only survived, it gained new strength at the close of the nineteenth century and into the twentieth century through the spiritual practices of Padre Martínez's followers—the Penitentes and the *Carmelitas.*

Although the Carmelitas were the female equivalent of the Penitentes, very little has been written about them, since they were always secluded and performed their penances separately.[46] According to one writer, the women would go up to the mountains or to some other secret place and flagellate themselves. They did not cut their backs, but they did whip them with cords.[47]

The Carmelitas, also sometimes called *Verónicas* and *Terceras* (Tertiaries), were often the wives and relatives of the Brothers, and like the Brothers they were dedicated to community service—ministering to the sick, helping the poor, and assisting in the burial of the dead.

Although some of the rituals of the Carmelitas were not as dramatic as those of the Penitentes, they were just as important to daily and religious life in New Mexico. According to Edwin Berry of Tomé, New Mexico:

El Encuentro *(The Encounter). Turn of the century, Taos, New Mexico. Courtesy Kit Carson Museum Foundation.*

These women dressed in black and they dedicated themselves to Jesus Christ. There were groups of Carmelitas in all of the neighboring villages. Interestingly, many of these women had the given name of Esquípula. Some served as *parteras* [midwives]. But they all sang alabados, never cut their hair, which they braided, and took a turn at playing the role of Verónica for the Passion Play. [The woman, chosen to play Verónica was always young and single.] The Carmelitas combined piety with humanitarian standards. They cared for the sick, fed the hungry, collected clothing and money for the poor, and often raised orphans. These women were also very secretive and never went out in public without covering their heads with a black shawl made of a heavy cloth. One of their many duties was to dress the old *santos* [images of saints] for Holy Week. The Carmelitas did their own penances and from the hair of the Verónicas they fashioned the wigs for the holy images.[48]

Jesusita Aragón, of Las Vegas, New Mexico, gave this account of her grandmother, María Dolores Córdova, who had been very involved as a member of the Carmelitas:

My grandmother, who was born in Corrales, New Mexico, was both a partera and a dedicated member of the Carmelitas in Trujillo, New Mexico. She, along with the other Carmelitas, attended meetings of the *sociedad* [society] at the San Isidro Church. They cleaned the church, dressed the santos, and sang alabados on feast days and wakes. On the 16th of July of every year, the Carmelitas observed the feast day of Our Lady of Carmel.

The Carmelitas were also known as *Las Hermanas* [the Sisters]. They were always involved in works of mercy and gladly wore the scapular of Our Lady of Carmel. Some of the single members of the order went on to enter the convent and became nuns. The order of

Carmelitas was very structured. They had officers, and each member was expected to perform a certain duty. They were very united, and when a member died they all gathered to hold a wake for their departed sister and sang their alabados. I remember when my grandmother was on her deathbed her fellow sisters placed dirt on the soles of her feet so she would be assured of a good and easy death.[49]

Touching dirt to the soles of the bare feet of a dying person was also a ritual of the Penitente Brothers.[50] In some instances an adobe brick was used.[51] This ritual can be considered part of the legacy of the Franciscans, who passed it on to the Carmelitas and the Fraternidad Piadosa de los Hermanos de Nuestro Padre Jesús Nazareno in New Mexico.

Procesión de las Carmelitas *(Carmelita procession). Nineteenth-century, New Mexico. Courtesy Museum of New Mexico, neg. no. 14757.*

Rituals and Ceremonies of the Brotherhood

Those who were primarily responsible for the preservation of the medieval customs and heritage of Spain in New Mexico were the members of the Fraternidad Piadosa de los Hermanos de Nuestro Padre Jesús Nazareno—the Penitentes. These men maintained a significant body of knowledge that was handed down from one generation to the next. The Penitentes were aided in this transmission of knowledge by the *auxiliarias de la Hermandad* (auxiliaries of the Brotherhood), the Carmelitas.

The Brotherhood in New Mexico was very well organized, consisting of the elder members, or *Los Hermanos de la Luz,* and *Los Hermanos de las Tinieblas* (Brothers of Darkness), sometimes called *Los Hermanos de Sangre* (Brothers of Blood). Los Hermanos de las Tinieblas were occasionally required to perform penitential activities, such as self-flagellation, over a period of five years before they were admitted as full-fledged members of the Brotherhood (Los Hermanos de la Luz).

The officers of each morada district were selected from Los Hermanos de la Luz and included El Hermano Mayor, the Elder Brother entrusted with the leadership of all members and activities; *El Hermano Celador,* the Brother responsible for the safekeeping, care, and repair of the

Procesión de las Carmelitas *(Carmelita procession). Turn of the century, Taos, Ne Mexico. Courtesy Kit Carson Museum Foundation.*

morada; *El Hermano Enfermero,* the Brother responsible for attending to the illnesses and injuries of his fellow members; *El Hermano Mandatorio,* the business manager, who handled all transactions, including transfers of money, food, and clothing to those in need; *El Hermano Secretario,* the scribe who recorded and preserved all of the information of value to the membership; and *El Maestro de Novicios,* the teacher of new candidates, who instructed them on the rules and regulations of the Brotherhood and orally examined them on the prayers and alabados, the knowledge of which was a prerequisite of membership.

The remaining Brothers performed various duties, such as *El Rezador,* the leader in reciting the rosary, prayers, and alabados; *El Pitero,* the flutist whose shrill, high-pitched notes signaled the start of a procession or religious ceremony or the recitation of a prayer or alabado verse; *El Santero,* the maker of holy images of Christ, Mary, and the saints; and those Brothers who fashioned the disciplinas, *matracas* (rosaries with hand-carved wood beads), and all of the other Penitente paraphernalia essential to the religious ceremonies and activities.

The Penitente Brothers were esteemed members of the mountain communities of northern New Mexico and southern Colorado. Among the male youths of the villages, it was considered quite an honor to be a Brother, and attaining the status of Brother signaled their passage from puberty to adulthood. A Penitente candidate had to be recommended for membership in the group. Once the candidate was accepted, rigorous training began, a major part of which consisted of the memorization of innumerable alabado stanzas and the recitation of these before El Hermano de

Novicios. The candidate also had to serve as a model in the community and was required to perform acts of mercy, charity, and humility.

The length of time it took to complete the initial training varied from individual to individual. After the period of training came the initiation. This solemn ceremony was held on the evening of Shrove Tuesday, the Tuesday immediately before Ash Wednesday. Each initiate, wearing cotton drawers and in bare feet, was conducted by one or more *Acompañaderos* (Attendants) to the morada, where he knocked soundly on the door, saying,

Dios toca en esta misión,
las puertas de su clemencia.

God knocks at this mission,
The doors of his clemency.

The Hermanos de la Luz within responded,

Penitencia, penitencia,
si quieres tu salvación.

Do penance, do penance,
If you want salvation.

The exchange continued back and forth:

San Pédro me abrirá la puerta,
bañandome con luz en el
nombre de María,
con el sello de Jesús
le pregunto a esta
confradía
¿Quién a esta casa da luz?
Jesús!

St. Peter will open the door,
Bathing me with light in the
name of Mary,
With the seal of Jesus.
I ask of this
confraternity
Who gives this house light?
Jesus!

¿Quién la llena de alegría?	Who fills it with joy?
María!	Mary!
¿Quién te llena de fé?	Who fills you with faith?
José!	Joseph!

Upon answering this final question, the Brothers in the morada opened the door, allowing the initiate to enter. Once inside he washed the feet of all those in attendance and recited an alabado asking for forgiveness. After this *El Sangrador* (the Bloodletter), cut three gashes down and three across the initiate's back with a *pedernal* (a piece of flint or glass), just shallow enough to avoid slicing into the muscles. The ceremony continued with the initiate saying,

Por el amor de Dios,	For the love of God,
las tres meditaciónes de	The three meditations of the
lapasión de Nuestro Señor.	Passion of our Lord.

El Sangrador, with a rawhide whip in hand, then delivered six strokes with his lash on the initiate's back—three on one side of the spine and three on the other.

After this the initiate entreated El Sangrador and was lashed with steadily more force as he uttered the following in a loud voice:

Por el amor de Dios,	For the love of God,
las cinco heridas de Cristo;	The five wounds of Christ;
Por el amor de Dios,	For the love of God,
las siete ultimas palabras;	The seven last words;
Por el amor de Dios,	For the love of God,
los cuarenta días en el desierto.	The forty days in the desert.

This generally ended the initiation ceremony. The candidate was then taken by *El Hermano Coadjutor* (the Helper) to El Hermano Enfermero, who treated his wounds with *inguente de romer,* (a medicinal ointment consisting of rosemary and lard or another base) and additional soothing herbs that accelerated the healing process. The conclusion of the ceremony signaled the beginning of forty days of *ejercicios* (exercises, or penances). The numerous isolated mountain moradas performed similar penitential rituals, although there were local differences regarding the severity of atonement for sin and the extent of self-infliction of pain and suffering.

In the mountains of Peñasco Blanco, near Mora, New Mexico, one Penitente walked barefoot each night of Holy Week from his morada to the church several miles away and back. Dressed only in long underwear, with the sleeves tied securely around his waist and with a black hood covering his head, he whipped his back at intervals as he traveled swiftly along a winding mountain trail. The entire penitential journey would normally take three to four hours to complete, since he periodically stopped to recite a sorrowful alabado verse and whip himself.

During the Lenten season, the Brothers met at their morada every day and night for a period of forty days. Family members and neighbors daily delivered food and provisions, and the Brothers, in return, would say a prayer and chant alabados for the purpose of intercession and protection of the donors. Anyone nearing the morada was escorted by *Hermanos Vigilantes* (Vigilant Brothers), who kept watch at various lookout points for undesirable intruders so as to be able to turn them away. This was nothing more than a precaution against curiosity seekers or those bent on ridiculing the Brotherhood's intensely religious ceremonies. Otherwise, the Brotherhood was open to anyone seeking comfort and salvation.

By the 1900s, there were approximately 135 active moradas, with several thousand members. Most of the moradas, like those in Las Trampas, Alcalde, Placita, Ranchitos (near the Española Valley), and Arroyo Seco, served as public chapels for the area. The chapel area of each morada was located in the front room, which contained an altar with *retablos* (altar paintings), handcarved santos, candles, and *ramilletes* (flowers cut from colored paper obtained from advertisements and magazines) or wildflowers and houseflowers dipped in wax. Most popular of the flowers were the beautiful pink, red, and yellow *rosas de Castilla* (roses of Castile), which were believed to have been brought over from Castilla, Spain, by Spanish ancestors. *Baras de San José* (hollyhocks, were also used extensively to decorate the altars.

Other items found in the chapel included *bancos,* handhewn pine benches, crucifixes, religious pictures in tin frames, wood or tin *nichos* (portable niches that housed religious images), and painted or carved stations of the cross. The inner room served as the penance room and usually contained *la carreta de la muerte* (death cart), *Palmilla disciplinas* (fibrous whips), handmade drums, washtubs, washbasins, lanterns, a small wood heater, and any other items deemed necessary for religious ceremonies.

The interior walls of the morada were whitewashed with *jaspe,* a gypsum powder mixed with water and natural adhesives. Sometimes colored stones were powdered and mixed in. On the ceilings usually hung a *manta*, a heavy canvas

Nuestra Señora de Guadalupe *(Our Lady of Guadalupe), by J. Guadalupe Góngora. Nineteenth-century engraving, Mexico. De Aragón family collection.*

cloth, pinned down at the corners to catch falling dust and debris. Powdered mica, or talco, was added to the adobe stucco of the exterior walls to make them shimmer in daylight or moonlight.

The Penitente Brothers were involved in the religious, social, and political life of their communities. They unswervingly referred to themselves as *Los Hispanos* (those of Hispanic descent), a term used solely in New Mexico and southern Colorado, and they proudly and passionately embraced their Spanish heritage. Contrary to current popular belief, the Penitentes, because of their acute isolation in mountainous regions, had negligible dealings with Mexico. They also kept relations with local Indian tribes to a bare minimum. Their saying was, *"Los Indios en su lugar, y nosotros en nuestro"* ("The Indians in their place, and we in ours")—an obvious allusion to the treaties signed between the Spanish government and the Indians that affirmed the autonomy of each culture.

Many of the Brothers worked in farming or as *ciboleros* (buffalo hunters), and these latter provided meat and buffalo hides to the villages. Others traveled yearly on La Borrega, the trail on which thousands of sheep were driven across the mountains to market. No matter how they made their living, the Penitentes never lost sight of what they believed to be their inherent duty: maintenance of the centuries-old traditions carried over from *Madre España* (Mother Spain).

A great deal of knowledge about the ancestors was contained in handwritten booklets passed from father to son. These booklets contained plays that were performed each season, and the presentation of these plays was an important way of educating the community in history, religion, and culture. Some of the plays dramatized stories from the Old Testament, such as the story of Adam and Eve, and some dramatized stories from the New Testament. These later included *San José* (St. Joseph); *Los Pastores* (The Shepherds); *Las Posadas* (The Christmas Inns); *Los Tres Reyes Magos* (The Three Wise Kings), *El Niño Perdido* (The Lost Child), which is about the appearance of Christ in the Temple and was presented during the spring; *Los Ciboleros* (The Buffalo Hunters); *Los Comanches,* a play about the Comanche Indians, *La Aparción de la Virjen de Guadalupe,* a dramatic account of the appearance of Our Lady of Guadalupe granted to Juan Diego; and *Los Moros* (The Moors), a dramatic presentation of the conflict between the Moors and the Christians.

Los Moros featured the Matachin dancers. According to a Hispanic tradition in northern New Mexico, the word *Matachin* is derived from *un matachinches,* a killer of disagreeable persons. The Matachin dance was imported from Spain during the colonization of the New World and was preserved in New Mexico. The Matachin dancers, through rhythmic movements and colorful costumes, vividly dramatized the defeat of the Moors and the triumph of Christianity over heretics and heresy. The bull dancer, reminiscent of Spain's love affair with matadors and the running of the bulls, plays a significant role in this spellbinding dance participated in by many of the Brothers. Some of the dancers carry a curious trident-like wooden board, symbolic of the Holy Trinity.

In the New World, Matachin dancers personified the Emperor Montezuma and the Aztec Indians being whipped into submission by the Spanish matador, with the aid of La

Matachine—*Acrylic and oil painting with painted frame, by Rosa María Calles.*

El Encuentro scene *(The Encounter). Las Carmelitas and Los Hermanos. Turn of the century, Taos, New Mexico. Courtesy Kit Carson Museum Foundation.*

Malinche, Cortés's interpreter. A young girl dressed in white was symbolic of the purity of the Christian struggle against heretic influences. The principal instruments, also typical of other Hispanic New Mexican dances, were the Spanish guitar and the violin. Most prevalent of the preserved dances were La Varsoviana, El Chotis, La Raspa, and La Jota, beautifully maintained and lovingly handed down from generation to generation.

Interestingly, the Penitentes did not allow circumcision among their male offspring. Even to this day, circumcision is not permitted in many Hispanic families, including some that do not have a tradition of membership in the Brotherhood. Many minor details such as this have been overlooked by scholars. As another example, Hispanos in New Mexico greeted each other, depending on the time of day, by saying, *"Buenos días le de Dios," "Buenas tardes le de Dios,"* or *"Buenas noches le de Dios"* ("May God grant you many good days," "May God grant you many good afternoons," "May God grant you many good nights"). Added to this was, *"¡Vaya con Dios!"* (Go with God!).

Each family had its own *altarcito* (little altar), where religious images, lighted candles, the family Bible, and other religious items were kept. The altarcito provided a place for meditation and prayer. Some families also maintained a *capillita* (little chapel), a small building replete with benches, santos, and other appropriate paraphernalia. Capillitas were available for anyone's use and were often the site of religious services.

The elder members of the community were addressed using the respectful title of *don* or *doña*, shortened forms of *de origen noble* (of noble origin). Many of the elders were *musicos* (musicians), who fashioned their own guitars and violins; *curanderas* and *parteras* (healers and midwives); and *cuentistas* (storytellers), who recounted parables and stories of faith, history, and sometimes romance.

The most important literary works were the mystery and the Passion Plays. *La Pasión,* a play dramatizing the trial and death of the Savior, was performed every year during Lent. The person portraying Christ was chosen from among the Penitente initiates. He typically had distinguished himself through good deeds, devotion, and masterful recitation of alabados.

The *Via Crucis* (Way of the Cross), which occurred during *La Cuaresma* (Lent), always began at the *camposanto* (cemetery) on Good Friday, but the Penitentes, prior to this, on the eve of Good Friday, held another important procession, the *Procesión de Maderos* (Procession of the Crosses). This procession started at the morada and was led by the Hermano Mayor and the Rezador. The path of the Rezador, the prayer leader, was lit by *Los Hermanos Compañeros,* who walked beside him carrying lanterns. Immediately behind them was the *Pitero,* the flutist, whose melodic cadence kept them in step, and the Brothers who carried the large, heavy wooden crosses. Each of the crossbearers had a companion to assist him. Several flagellants wearing black hoods and black trunks followed the crosses, and behind them were Las Carmelitas, the penitent women with their long black dresses and black shawls.

The procession started with the Rezador singing a verse from *Dios Toca en Esta Misión* (God Knocks at This Mission). The group periodically stopped on their way to the Calvario (Penitente calvary, usually located three hundred yards or more away), and another verse would be recited. The Hermano Mayor signaled for the procession to continue by rattling his matraca (a wood rattle with ratchets) at the end of each verse. The procession was concluded at the *Calvario* with the reenactment of the Crucifixion. Three of the Carmelitas played the parts of the three Marys: Mary, the mother of Christ; Mary Magdalene; and the "other" Mary. After this, everyone returned to the morada for *Las Tinieblas*. Las Tinieblas, which commemorated the period following Christ's death on the cross, was led by El Hermano Mayor, who recited the alabado litany for the villagers at the morada. While El Hermano Mayor chanted verses describing Christ's desertion by the apostles, fifteen candles on a high, triangular wooden candelabra were extinguished one by one after each verse until all were put out. The altar cloth was torn at the point of darkness, symbolizing the earthquake after Christ died. Sheer pandemonium followed, representing the Last Judgment Day. A scene of terrifying realism was created through the sounds of clanking chains and matracas; the banging of *jumates y cucharas* (saucepans and spoons), *cajetes* (metal washtubs), *lavaderos* (washboards), and *bandejas* (metal washbasins); and the steady thud of the Penitente whips. The Pitero's high-pitched notes combined with the sorrowful alabado laments and the heartrending cries of the women and children.

The chaos subsided in less than a half hour, and dead silence followed. El Hermano Mayor then led prayers *(sudarios)* for the living, the dead, the souls in Purgatory, those at war, and so on. Noise making and then silence followed each sudario. A potluck meal was served at a home nearby at the conclusion of the ceremony. The fare included *frijoles con quelites y cebolla* (beans with spinach and onions), *torta de huevo* (beaten eggs with red chile), *buñuelos* (fried yeasted bread), *panocha* (wheat pudding), *posole* (a stew consisting of hominy, chile, and pork), and *natillas* (egg pudding), which were the traditional New Mexican Lenten dishes. The Penitentes returned to their morada, and the Carmelitas returned to their meeting place to hold an all-night *velorio* (vigil) for the sorrowful Blessed Mother, represented by a large wooden image.

The *Encuentro,* the enactment of the meeting of Jesus and his mother on his way to Calvary, took place on Good Friday. Four of the Veronicas carried the statue of Mary while a fifth carried the *Rostro de Jesús*, a reproduction of the cloth imprint of Christ's face. *Las Verónicas* were younger members of the Carmelitas whose duty and honor it was to sacrifice their long, beautiful hair for use in making the santos (the hair used had to be a young girl's hair never before cut) and to care for these religious images. The Penitentes and Carmelitas met at a certain location carrying statues of Mary and Christ on wooden litters. The lead Veronica immediately went up to the statue of Christ, and in a ritual recalling the deed of St. Veronica, she wiped the face of Christ three times. Then the cheeks of the statues of Mary and Christ were touched together in the El Encuentro, the encounter and embrace of mother and son. El Hermano Mayor sang an alabado of great sorrow, which introduced the next procession.

The Via Crucis started at the cemetery, with the Rezador and Pitero leading the way. Two Brothers carrying crosses were followed by flagellants; Hermanos de la Luz carrying crosses were followed by flagellants; Hermanos de la Luz

La Pasión en el Monte Calvario *(The Passion at a Penitente Mount Calvary). Nineteenth-century, New Mexico. Courtesy Museum of New Mexico, neg. no. 125551.*

carrying the *Santo Entierro*, a painted wood container with openings housing a wooden image of Christ with moveable arms to be hung up on a cross; Carmelitas; and numerous other men, women, and children. The latter group carried a large crucifix, a statue of Mary, and many images (tin-framed pictures of the saints or wood retablos). The entire gathering stopped every fifty feet or so on their way to the morada to pray and sing sorrowful alabados of the Passion.

Other crossbearers replaced the initial two when the procession reached the morada. Some of the Hermanos at the morada had pieces of *cizaña* (tumbleweed) strapped to their backs, chests, and arms. On reaching the Calvario, the crossbearers prostrated themselves at the foot of the Calvary crosses, and the crosses they were carrying were placed on their backs for a few minutes while the Pitero played his flute and the Rezador chanted alabado verses.

Meanwhile at the morada, the chosen *Cristo* was led out of the building dressed in white *calzoncillos* (long underpants) and with a black cloth tied around his head. After being laid on a cross that had a platform to rest his feet, the Cristo was securely tied to it. A white sheet was then wrapped around him from head to foot and tied down so that only his arms and covered head were exposed. The entire cross was then lifted upright and slid into a hole that had been previously dug for this purpose. El Hermano Mayor and some of the other brothers at this time wore *rosas de Castilla,* thorn crowns which dug into their heads and temples. After twenty-five to thirty minutes of silence, El Hermano Mayor announced, *"Cristo ha muerto, y todos son salvados. Dale tu alma, la cual el pide."* ("Christ has died, and everyone is saved. Give him your soul for which he is calling.")

El Hermano Mayor's announcement signaled the conclusion of the Penitente Passion ceremonies. The Cristo was lowered down and untied from the cross, and all went into the morada. A final Lenten gathering of the Hermanos, the Carmelitas, and their families and friends took place. They shared a light meal, the ritual end to their strict fast.

The Brothers returned home, but their duties did not thereby come to an end. They were expected to perform benevolent deeds throughout the year. Los Hermano Mayores, for example, worked at settling disputes within their communities. The elder Penitentes acted as counselors and, being patriotic and law-abiding men, served as examples for everyone around them. All the Brothers played the role of teachers, preserving culture, traditions, and history and assisted in the maintenance of law and order. Also, they and their families often took in orphans and collected clothing and food for the poor. Last but not least, the Brothers preserved the alabado hymns, lovingly passing them down from generation to generation with the idea of keeping the Brotherhood and the beauty of their faith alive.

Monte Calvario *(Penitente Mount Calvary). El Cerro, New Mexico. Photograph by Lucía de Aragón.*

Penitente Arts: Tradition and Innovation

The overall organization of the Penitente Brotherhood reflects the religious spirit of the Spanish people. The religious art of the confraternity is also intrinsically linked with this spirit, although its roots can be traced back to early Christian iconography.

Christian art, including the New Mexican santero folk art, has always played an important role in the worship of God. Imagery fulfilled some of the aesthetic needs of the worshippers and helped activate their faith. During the early centuries of Christianity, a type of art that was distinctively Christian gradually developed. In the catacombs and private homes of Christians, the familiar forms of Roman pagan decoration were transformed by new themes motivated by Christian inspiration. New symbols (for example, fish, laurel leaves, crosses, shells, and rosettes) associated with the primitive Christian Church were added to existing Roman motifs.

In the year 313, by the ordinance of Licinius, public veneration was finally allowed. Frescoes and mosaics displaying Christ, Mary, the apostles, and the patriarchs of the Old Testament were openly exhibited.[52] When persecution of the Christians ended and Christianity became the official religion, early Christian art evolved into Byzantine art, which, though still symbolic, was more representational.

This type of art, which originated in Constantinople, was derived from early Greek and Christian art and is characterized by the use of lavish color and florid design.

In the late sixth century, crucifixes—crosses that include a representation of Jesus—began to occur in manuscripts and on private and public monuments. The Syrian codex of the Gospels, produced around 586, contains the earliest known image of the crucified Christ. Crucifixes also made their appearance on the altars of the Byzantine churches and the Syrian monasteries.

In the early Middle Ages, illuminated manuscripts of an extremely high artistic level were created in the monasteries. The miniaturists who painted them often copied contemporary frescoes and earlier frescoes painted on the walls of the catacombs. As a result, a more ascetic ideal developed: The faces were depicted with more intense expressions, and the figures had taut outlines. There was also a shift from the portrayal of the resurrected Christ to the portrayal of the suffering Christ. The motive may have been to lead believers away from materialism to an acceptance of suffering. This was the era of the Black Death, which had a profound impact on artistic trends.

Devotion to the suffering Christ was manifested not only in the art but also in the actions of the people. Christians engaged in self-abasement to demonstrate their acceptance of suffering and their willingness to sacrifice themselves for others—a willingness that mirrored the active compassion of God.

The artists of the Middle Ages grappled with the problem of forcefully portraying the suffering of ordinary humans as well as the suffering of Jesus Christ. Death was depicted as a

Crucifijo *(Crucifix) from Morada, New Mexico. Courtesy Museum of New Mexico, neg. no. 705.*

La Vírgen y el Santo Niño. *Baroque Mother and Child, polychromed and gilded wood sculpture. Nineteenth-century, Spain.*

skeleton, and the theme of death seizing all men, from emperors to peasants, became popular throughout Europe.

The European representation of death evolved over time. The death figure was first shown with a scythe, but in later renditions the figure holds a bow and arrow. Some sixteenth-century woodcut engravings depicted death with a scythe, a bow and arrow, and a hatchet.[53]

Many of the sculptors working in Spain during the Renaissance were either Spaniards trained in Italy or Italians commissioned to do artworks for Spanish churches and religious groups. However, in the first half of the sixteenth century, a national school of sculpture developed.[54] The sculptors of this school worked within the confines of the Italian High Renaissance, but they contributed to the genesis of the Spanish Baroque, with its idealized realism and emotionality.

During the latter part of the sixteenth century, Juan Martínez Montañés, a sculptor who had a tremendous impact on Spanish art, began his career in Granada. Montañés is considered the greatest master of Spanish polychrome religious sculpture, and Murillo and Velásquez are counted among the many admirers of his work. His images are characterized by the naturalness of their appearance and the severity of their expression (Jesus crucified was the most common motif of his religious sculptures). In addition to sculpting, he also designed and painted *reredos*, the ornamental screens located behind altars.

Many of the works produced by Montañés were destined for use in the New World, including one complete retablo sent to a convent in Panama and over fifty carved tabernacles installed in churches across South America.

Followers of Montañés included Juan de Mesa, who was commissioned by the penitent brotherhoods in Spain to produce figures for use in Holy Week processions. The primary statue was always a representation of the tortured Christ rendered in explicit anatomical detail. It was typically life-size and had jointed arms so it could be carried in a procession, tied to a mock pillar, pegged to a cross to simulate crucifixion, and, after removal from the cross, placed in a wooden coffin with openings for easy viewing. These sculptures were designed to engender compassion and repentance among those in the crowd.

After Mesa's death, Alonso Cano remained the only major artist to carry on the sculptural tradition of Montañés in Seville, although he spent most of his life as a painter. Cano had a classic Baroque style, but the work of his students tended to be more dramatic.

In the New World, a tradition in religious polychrome art was established and carried on through the training of younger artists. Guilds made their way across the Atlantic, and soon native sculptors were fulfilling the need for religious images in the expanding colonies. The first colonists to enter New Mexico brought sacred images with them. These images, including the popular *Nuestra Señora de la Conquista* (Our Lady of the Conquest), were mainly produced in Spain. During the Pueblo Revolt of 1680, most of the sacred images were destroyed by the Indians, but a group of Spaniards were able to transport the polychrome statue of Our Lady of the Conquest to El Paso del Norte.

Soon after the reconquest of New Mexico, Franciscan friars made santos (sacred images) in the classic Baroque style to use as ornaments for their chapels and churches.

El Crucifijo *(The Crucifix), by Pedro Frésquez. Eighteenth- century, New Mexico.*

Along with several anonymous friars was one identified as Fray Andrés García, born in La Puebla de los Ángeles, México. Fray García, who was stationed in New Mexican missions for thirty-two years, carved pulpits, altar rails and screens, and religious images and also painted pictures on wood panels. Franciscans, however, were not the only creators of semiacademic art in eighteenth-century New Mexico. Several wooden figures and pictures were made by Captain Bernardo de Miera y Pacheco, a professional soldier. Miera y Pacheco was born near Burgos, Spain, and spent twelve years in El Paso before moving with his family to Santa Fe, where he lived for thirty- one years.

The work of Fray García and Miera y Pacheco stimulated the indigenous santero school of New Mexico.[55] and regional artists in the eighteenth century continued working in the same tradition. However, in the early nineteenth century, Pedro Antonio Fresquíz (1785–1831), of Las Truchas, probably the first native-born santero, began to produce santos in a folk art style. Other New Mexican folk artists also created works to meet the needs of the churches, and these same artists were commissioned by the Penitente Brotherhood to produce santos for their Holy Week processions.

The Franciscans, because of their focus on ministering to the Indians, often neglected the spiritual requirements of the Spanish settlers. The void created by such neglect was filled by the lay religious associations, to which most of the settlers already belonged. Initially, the only two associations were the Third Order of St. Francis and the lay order of the Carmelites. The Pious Fraternity of the Brothers of Father Jesus the Nazarene and the Carmelitas, which steadily grew in popularity and strength, were basically extensions of these two medieval orders.

The penitential groups operating in territories with a strong Franciscan presence were supervised by the friars, and the relationship between the groups and the friars continued for well over two hundred years. The friars worked in the missions establishing schools, instructing the Indians (and nearby settlers when possible) in arts and crafts, spreading the gospel, and training their Spanish assistants to continue their work.

Spanish lay followers who had been instructed by the friars and had learned the basic skills necessary to produce local arts and crafts carried on the established traditions in religious art. The New Mexican santeros had to be resourceful since they were required to manufacture their own painting tools, grounds, pigments, glues, and varnishes.

Many of the lay santeros working in New Mexico were prolific, and their work was highly regarded by the people. These staunchly religious men sought to spread the faith through their work, and many Hispanics throughout New Mexico considered the images they created to be miraculous. Several of the santeros were active members of the Brotherhood, and it was their duty to provide religious images for the moradas and nearby churches. Sometimes santeros were commissioned to make santos for private homes, but mostly their work was intended for use by the penitential associations.

The santos were of two types: *bultos,* which are traditional statues in the round, and *retablos,* which are pictures of the saints painted on wood panels. Christ in agony continued to be a leading motif, but the New Mexican santos became more starkly realistic. Some of them had actual human teeth, human fingernails, and human hair. They

San Antonio de Padua *(St. Anthony of Padua). Nineteenth-century, New Mexico. De Aragón family collection.*

were colored using paints made from natural materials and had leather shoulder joints so they could be easily fastened to and removed from a cross during the dramatization of the episodes of the Passion.

Death was portrayed as a grotesque skeleton with a horsehair wig and obsidian or mother-of-pearl eyes and was dressed in a black robe with a hood that covered its head. The image was placed in a wooden cart[56] and held a hatchet or bow and arrow. The overall effect was intended to shock viewers into a state of repentance. The inclusion of the image of death in penitential processions was integral to the purpose of the Holy Week ceremonies.[57]

Besides Pedro Antonio Fresquíz, the most active Penitente santeros included Antonio Silva (active 1790 to circa 1810), Antonio Molleno (1804 to circa 1845), José Rafael Aragón (1826–1855), Miguel Herrera (circa 1870–1880), and Juan Ramón Velásquez (circa 1870–1907). It is interesting to note that José Benito Ortega (active from 1870 to circa 1907) painted the body of the crucified Christ in a bluish tinge. The use of blue to paint Christ was of iconographic significance among Italian primitives, but the practice was discarded after Giotto (circa 1266–1337). How this practice came to be revived in isolated New Mexico is a complete mystery.

New Mexico santeros fashioned their unique santos out of pine, cottonwood, and cottonwood root. The hands, arms, legs, feet, torsos, and heads of the images were usually carved separately and then joined together with dowel pins, in contrast to those produced elsewhere in the Spanish- speaking world which were usually carved from a single piece of wood. Sometimes a figure was carved down to the waist and attached to a wooden tripod that was itself attached to a base. The tripod was then covered with leather, muslin, or cotton cloth dipped in a *yeso* (gypsum gesso) mixture to form a dress or a skirt.

The yeso was always baked in an *estufa* (wood cooking stove), ground to a powder with a mortar and pestle, and slowly cooked in an iron pot with water and animal glue to a creamy consistency. After cooling, the yeso was applied to the carved figures as a base for painting. The yeso could also be built up in layers to compensate for any problems or errors in carving. The santero produced their paints using local minerals, such as hematites, limonite, cochineal, logwood, and vermilion. They also used yellows derived from plants and roots, including chamisa, dock, and mountain mahogany root. Ground up stove ashes and soot provided the pigment for making black. Home made *jaspe* house paints were sometimes also used for greens and yellows. The completed images received a coating of egg white or melted *trementina* (pine resin) to give them a varnished effect.

The distinctively New Mexican santos had a personality of their own and closely resembled the local people, who often served as models for the artists. Cleofas Jaramillo recalled in her book, *Shadows of the Past,* that her Aunt Soledad served as a model for an image of *Nuestra Señora de la Soledad* (Our Lady of Solitude). The santero Juan Miguel Herrera from Arroyo Hondo also wanted her mother to pose for a statue of *Nuestra Señora del Rosario* (Our Lady of the Rosary). Cleofas Jaramillo wrote that Herrera often played a handmade violin at weddings and other social gatherings. He also led the singing at the church and morada.

In the 1870s and 1880s, Herrera (who sometimes worked with his brother Candelario) produced Santo Entierro images of Christ that had the jaws set with springs

San Isidro Labrador *(St. Isidore the Plowman). Nineteenth-century, New Mexico. De Aragón family collection.*

in order to simulate a person in his last agony. Stark realism was also attained in crucifixes by creating openings in the side of Christ's body from which red colored water or animal blood could flow. Penitente members occasionally served as models for Herrera's images of Christ.

The work of Antonio Silva, one of the pioneer santeros from Tomé, embellished the Penitente moradas of Tomé, Adelino, El Cerro, La Ladera, Casa Colorada, La Joya, Sabinal, Los Chavez, Belen, and Los Lunas. In fact, the works of the Sangre de Cristo santeros were often brought south to the mountain villages of the Manzanos, and those of the Manzano santeros made their way up north. One of the most popular of the northern santeros was Antonio Molleno, called the "chile painter" because of his red-chile-pod-like designs. Molleno, who became a master of simplification, was influenced, like many other New Mexican santeros, by the designs found on the early wallpaper that made its way to New Mexico along the Santa Fe Trail.

Striking facial features such as an aquiline or pug nose, slightly crossed eyes, a protruding jaw, and high cheekbones, frequently appear in the work of the New Mexico santeros. José Benito Ortega's images tended to have long thin noses and oval faces. He manufactured his santos for the Penitente moradas of Mora, San Miguel, Taos, Santa Fe, and Union counties as well as for moradas in southern Colorado. Ortega's santos were dressed in the fashions of the day (for example, his female saints wore the black pegged boots that became popular in New Mexico). He was perhaps the most prolific of the santeros who worked during the peak of Penitente activity in New Mexico.

Nuestra Señora del Rosario *(Our Lady of the Rosary), by José Benito Ortega. Nineteenth-century, Mora, New Mexico. Courtesy Rev. George Salazár collection.*

The santos created by Ortega, along with those produced by José Rafael Aragón of Córdova, whose santos exhibited elongated bodies and bright colors, and Juan Ramon Velásquez, whose innovations included the use of enamel house paints, were used for *Velorio de Santo* celebrations. During this time some of the santos from the morada or other nearby sources would be taken to a host home. The Penitente Rezador led prayers in honor of the saints for those in attendance and sang *canticos* throughout the evening. At midnight everyone enjoyed a meal that included *chile caribe, calabacitas* (fried green pumpkins), and *arroz dulce con pasas* (sweet rice with raisins).

All of the moradas were dedicated to patron saints. The santeros were commissioned to create saint images keeping in mind the special reverence the Penitentes held for that particular saint. Other santos, such as the *Santo Niño* (the Holy Christ Child), were used for religious dramas like *Los Pastores,* the miracle play of the shepherds performed at Christmas time. A general favorite was the image of *San Ysidro* (Saint Isidore the Plowman), which was carried out into the fields in procession in the hope of ensuring a bountiful crop. The popular demand for santos kept the santeros busy creating images for feast day celebrations, Holy Week processions, and religious plays.

The Carmelitas were also involved in artistic activity. They produced among other things, embroidered altar cloths decorated with skulls for the moradas as well as many other beautifully embroidered cloths adorned with religious representations. They made straw-inlaid crosses, and decorated furnishings with straw inlay. In a few cases, the women created hide paintings using tanned elk dyes and indigo. They also wove jerga wool floor coverings for the moradas, the churches, and their homes on handmade looms, using weaving techniques that had been handed down from generation to generation since the time their ancestors left Spain. The dominant design among the jergas, of which few examples are extant, was the crenelated parapet dating from the Spanish Christian/Moorish wars.

Many of the monastic saints are found represented in New Mexico's santero folk art. *Santiago* (St. James), who was a common subject in Spanish art, was also popular among the santeros. In New Mexican retablos, he usually appears bearded on horseback, holds a spear or sword, and is trampling a field of Moorish bodies. The depiction of Santiago as the warrior saint of Spain spurred on the reconquest of Spain and the conquest of the Americas.

New Mexican religious art also includes representations of *San Antonio Abad* (St. Anthony of Egypt), *San Bernardo* (St. Bernard of Clairvaux), *San Francisco de Asís* (St. Francis of Assisi), *San Buenaventura* (St. Bonaventure), *San Gerónimo* (St. Jerome), *San Vicente Ferrer* (St. Vincent Ferrer), and *San Damiano* (St. Damian). All of these saints played an important part in the history of the church and its penitential movements and ultimately inspired the Penitentes of New Mexico.

The chief examples of Penitente architecture were the moradas, which functioned as chapter meeting houses and chapels. A typical morada was a long adobe building with massive walls and no windows. It was basically a rectangular box with one end blunted and buttressed by a belltower constructed of stones. An altar was located in the interior, and the holy images, together with a skull,[58] were placed alongside it.

Nuestra Señora de la Rosa *(Our Lady of the Rose). Polychromed wood sculpture with leather, silver, and turquoise, by Ray John de Aragón.*

The predominant requests for religious images for morada altars were for representations of the Holy Mother of Christ. The special reverence the Penitentes had for her is shown by these lines from an early nineteenth-century alabado:

Un ángel desde el cielo	An angel from on high
tendió sus bellas alas,	Spread its beautiful wings,
y del risueño oriente	And from the bright East
llegando a la morada,	Arriving at the morada
sus puertas abre, y luego	Opened the doors, and then
con júbilo así exclama:	With jubilance exclaimed:
"Despierta galana,	"Awaken beautiful dawn [in reference to Mary]
y esparce en todo el mundo	And spread throughout the world
raudal de luces claras."	Abundant lucid light."

The cross is the most important emblem of Christ in the Christian faith. In the early days of Christianity, when the church was persecuted, the cross was used only in secret. It was disguised so as to avoid detection of Christian centers by nonmembers. One of the ways the cross was altered was by the addition of bars of different lengths placed horizontally or diagonally along the vertical bars. Curiously, the Penitentes in New Mexico also used crosses designed in this manner, including the crosses they carried in their processions and the crosses they placed on the interior walls of their homes and moradas. It was not until the fifth century that the persecution of Christians ceased and the open use of unaltered crosses spread. It is possible that the Penitentes, because of their condemnation by church officials, felt the need to disguise the holy cross in much the same way as the early Christians.

Santo Niño de Atocha *(The Holy Child of Atocha). Polychromed pine sculpture and nicho, by Ray John de Aragón.*

Another Old World custom which was preserved and expanded in New Mexico was the use of straw inlay to decorate black-painted crosses, frames, chests, wooden boxes, coffins, and furniture with exquisite geometric designs. This craft of Moorish ancestry reached new heights in New Mexico and was integrated beautifully with the artistic legacy of the Penitentes. Material goods were a luxury so nothing was wasted, everything was put to use. In fact, magazine pictures were cut out and used to wallpaper their homes. New Mexico santeros were also able to make extensive use of hammered-out tin which came from discarded containers left by the American traders along the Santa Fe Trail. With cut tin cans they created striking floral and geometric designs on crowns for their santos and for the nichos (niches) used to house them. Tin was also used to frame religious engravings brought into the territory and for lanterns, and other candleholders used to light the interior of the moradas or for use in Penitente nocturnal processions. This form of artwork also gained widespread popularity outside the borders of New Mexico.

New Mexico artists were able to synthesize the religious traditions of medieval Catholicism and adapt them to the harsh land of New Mexico. While religious art in other Spanish-speaking areas underwent profound changes in both style and content, Baroque sculpture, with its medieval aspects, endured in isolated New Mexico well into the nineteenth century and has survived as folk art even into the twentieth century—which is not to say that New Mexican Hispanic culture lacked its own special characteristics. New Mexico Hispanics were very progressive and blazed trails in all walks of life. Many became nationally and international-

San Rafael Arcángel *(St. Raphael the Archangel). Polychromed wood sculpture and nicho, by Ray John de Aragón. Courtesy Museum of International Folk Art Collection.*

ly recognized artists, such as Patrocinio Barela of Taos, who produced his unique style of santos and death carts for Penitente moradas in the 1940s. The newer artists followed a tradition established by their santero forebears, but they bridged the gap between folk art and fine art.

Nuestra Señora de la Luz. *(Our Lady of the Light), by J. Guadalupe Góngora. Nineteenth-century engraving, Mexico. De Aragón family collection.*

Evolution of the Alabado Hymns

Vamos fieles, todos juntos	All faithful let us go together
alabando a nuestro Dios,	Praising our God,
en quien creemos y esperamos	Whom we believe in and wait for
y amamos de corazón.	And love with all our heart.
Alabemos a María	We all praise Mary
en su limpia concepción	In her most pure conception,
y a José su casto esposo,	And also Joseph her chaste husband,
nuestro amante protector.	Who is our loving protector.

The New Mexican alabados are religious hymns that serve to praise or glorify Christ, Mary (Jesus's mother), or the saints. Some of these hymns begin with the words *alabado sea* (praised be). Alabado is the past participle of *alabar* (to praise), which derives from the Latin *alapari* or the Greek *lapidsoo,* meaning to glorify, or from *allaudare,* composed from *ad* and *laudare,*[59] meaning to praise. By the thirteenth century, *alabado* came to mean specifically a hymn praising or celebrating the Passion of Christ. The original thirteenth-century meaning has only been preserved in New Mexico. The alabados embody a profound faith in God. This same type of religious faith was also expressed in the early works of Spanish literature, such as the twelfth-century *Poema de Mío Cid* (The Poem of El Cid) and the thirteenth-century *Poema de Fernán Gonzáles,* which mentioned the religious fervor of the Spanish people:

Desque los españoles a
Cristo conoscieron,
desque en la su ley
bautismo recibieron,
nunca en otra ley tornarse
quisieron,
mas por guardar de
aquesto muchos males
sufrieron.

Ever since the time the
Spaniards discovered Christ,
Ever since by law they
received baptism,
Never did they want to return to
any other law,
Instead, in defense of
this right, they
suffered.

During the Middle Ages, Spanish religious ballads, narrative poems or songs of popular origin in short stanzas, often with a refrain, enjoyed a widespread vogue. They displayed a burst of love intended to praise God, Mary, or the saints and to raise the thoughts and affections of the faithful. They were meant to strengthen the sentiments and virtues that holy persons or occasions ought to inspire.

Religious ballads can be traced back to the very cradle of Christianity. They were sung in the homes of the faithful and in the catacombs. They evolved from even earlier hymns that were sung by the Hebrews when they started their journey to the Promised Land. The words the Hebrews used came directly from the Book of Psalms in the Old Testament. The Hebrew men and women chanted the hymns in unison or in antiphony. In the latter case, one group might intone, "I will lift up mine eyes unto the hills, from whence cometh my help." The second group would answer, "My help cometh from the Lord, which made heaven and earth."[60] Early Christian hymns expressed the faith and fortitude of those who sang them. These hymns were chanted in unison, and the rhythm used is known as "free rhythm" since it is unrestrained by a fixed rhythm or pattern of accentuation. In short, the hymns were intoned using a melodious form of speaking.[61]

In A.D. 600, Pope Gregory I introduced a system of eight "modes," or scales, for chanting the liturgical hymns. These were similar to the nonmetrical Greek modes used for words in unison. The Gregorian chants (named after Pope Gregory I) were descended from the early hymns of the Greeks and Hebrews and embodied a prose rhythm or free-verse rhythm. They had a close similarity to the lost monophonic[62] musical art of ancient Greece, Palestine, and Syria.[63] Two other events had a substantial effect on the evolution of the Penitente alabados. One was the adoption of the Byzantine chants by the church, and the second was the invasion of the Iberian Peninsula by the Moors.

Many popular Spanish *cantos* (canticles) are deeply rooted in the civilization of ancient Byzantium. The cantos were adopted into daily use by the Spanish church in the eleventh century. During this period, the Roman liturgy was also introduced. The most typical of the Byzantine chants are related to the alabados with regard to the following elements: the tonal modes of the primitive system: the division and subdivision of harmonizing notes, the absence of a metric rhythm within the line of melody, and the richness of modulating inflection.

Some of these same elements occur in Moorish chants. However, Moorish influences in Spain postdate the Catholic

Church's adoption of the Byzantine chants. The Arabs and Moors apparently did no more than reform some of the ornamental lines common to the Oriental and Persian chant systems. Another important factor was the development of Christian lyric poetry. In the thirteenth century, a group of poets appeared who wrote hymns of the Passion in the same style as the alabados. For example, Philippe the Chancellor (circa 1160–1236) composed a series of hymns to the Virgin and Mary Magdalene that manifest a childlike simplicity and devotion. Giovanni di Fidanza (1221–1274), better known as St. Bonaventure, wrote *The Tree of Life,* a devotional work celebrating the Passion of the Lord. He also wrote a beautiful Passion hymn titled *Recordare Sanctae Crucis* (Remember the Holy Way of the Cross).[64]

In the late Middle Ages, Latin hymn writing declined from the high level it had attained in the twelfth and thirteenth centuries. However, some hymns of this period are remarkable for their carefully cultivated form and their tone of deep piety, such as those of the fourteenth-century Franciscan poet Jacopone da Todi. Da Todi was the author of the world- famous *Stabat Mater Dolorosa,* which portrays the Virgin Mary at the Crucifixion. *Stabat Mater Dolorosa* was originally intended for private devotion; this hymn was included in many fifteenth-century books of prayer and by the end of the century was incorporated into the liturgy. Da Todi's hymns became the foundation of the laudistic tradition of hymns of praise or honor. The literature of the Middle Ages includes a substantial quantity of religious poetry, narrative as well as lyric. One of the greatest Spanish poets of the period was Gonzalo de Berceo (circa 1196–1264), considered by some to be the father of Castilian poetry. De

Nuestra Señora del Refugio *(Our Lady of the Refuge), by J. Guadalupe Góngora. Nineteenth-century engraving, Mexico. De Aragón family collection.*

Berceo was associated with the Benedictine monastery of San Millán de la Cogolla in La Rioja, where he was probably a notary assigned to the abbot. He was the author of nine devotional works composed in *cuaderna vía,* a Spanish verse form originating in the twelfth century. *Cuadernos* are monorhymic lines systematically arranged in groups of four.

In *Tu, Christe que luz eres,* De Berceo refers to Christ as the "divine light," which calls to mind the New Mexican alabado *Por ser mi divina luz* (You Are My Divine Light):

Tu Christe que luz eres,	You, Christ, who are the light
que alumnas el día,	That illumines the day,
que tuelles las tinieblas,	That takes away the darkness
faceslas ir su via,	And guides the way,
bien creo que luz eres,	I truly believe that you are the light,
lumne de alma mía,	Light of my soul,
e que predigas lumne e toda bien fetria.	And that you preach of light and all that is good.

In *Loores de Nuestra Señora,* a poem that praises Mary, mother of Christ, as the instrument of redemption, De Berceo reminds all Christians to be penitent:

Los qui somos xpianos e en xpo creemos,	Those of us who are Christians and who believe in Christ,
si estas visiones scusarlas queremos,	To free ourselves from bad visions,
meioremos las vidas, penitencias tomemos,	To make our lives better, penitence we must do,
ganaremos la gloria, el mal escusaremos.	We then will win glory and shake away evil.

De Berceo's *Duelo de la Virgen el día de la pasión de su Hijo* (Sorrow of the Virgin on the Day of the Passion of Her Son) contains an account of the Crucifixion as experienced by the mother of Christ. The poem is addressed to St. Bernard of Clairvaux and appears to have been derived from the latter's *Liber de Passione Christi et Doloribus et Planctibus Matris Eius* (Book of the Passion of Christ and the Sorrow and Lamentation of His Mother). It includes a conversation between St. Bernard and the mother of Christ on her son's Passion, followed by an account, in Mary's own words, of his death:

Con sabia del mi Fijo,	Because of the anguish of my son,
mi padre, mi señor,	My father, my Lord,
mi lumne, mi confuerto, mi salud, mi pastor,	My light, my comfort, my health, my pastor,
mi vida, mi conseio, mi gloria, mi dulzor,	My life, my consolation, my glory, my sweetness,
nin aviá de vida nin cobdicia nin sabor.	I had no will nor desire to go on living.

In the late Middle Ages, it became common to write about the sorrow of Mary and the Passion of Christ. For example, Juan Ruiz (circa 1283–1350), Arcipreste de Hita, wrote *De la Pasión de Nuestro Señor Jesucristo,* the verses of which are reminiscent of the alabados of New Mexico:[65]

En su faz escupieron	On his face they spit
del cielo claridad,	From the clearness of the sky,
de espinas lo coronan	With thorns he was crowned
con mucha crueldad;	With extreme cruelty;

en la cruz lo subieron,	On the cross he was raised,
no tenían piedad.	They had no piety.
Tomemos de estas	We take from all these wounds
llagasdolor y grán pesar.	Great pain and so much sorrow.
1064	1064
Con clavos le clavaron	With nails they nailed
las manos y los pies,	His hands and his feet,
y su sed abrevaron	And his thirst they quenched
con vinagre y con hiel;	With vinegar and gall;
las llagas que le hicieron	The wounds which they made
son más dulces que miel	Are much sweeter than honey
para los que tenemos	For those of us who firmly
firme esperanza en él.	Place our hope in him.
1065	1065
En la cruz fue muerto,	On the cross he met his death,
herido y llagado,	Wounded and injured,
y después fue abierto	And after they did open
con lanza su costado:	With a lance his side:
por este pecho abierto	Through this opened breast
el mundo fue salvado.	The world was saved.
A los que en El creemos	Those of us who believe in him
el nos quiera salvar.	He will want to save.
1066	1066

Additional authors who wrote on the Passion during the fifteenth century include Fray Yñigo de Mendoza, Juan Alvarez Gato, Juan de Padilla, Yñigo López de Mendoza, Marqués de Santillana, and many anonymous poets. Samples of their poetry can be found in the Appendix.

It is clear that a strong connection exists between the New Mexican Penitente alabados and traditional Spanish Christian poetry. In fact, the alabado *Estabas, madre dolorosa* is a version of the medieval Latin hymn *Stabat Mater* and follows the tradition of early Franciscan spirituality. Another alabado, *Por el rastro de la sangre,* which is known in numerous versions throughout Spanish America, can be traced to a hymn published by Juan López de Ubeda in his book *Vergel de flores divinas,* printed in Alcala de Henares in 1582. Although portions of the sixteenth-century version differ, they exhibit an overall similarity. This is not surprising, since New Mexico was an isolated land that maintained Old World customs even while the rest of the Spanish-speaking world was undergoing social, political, and cultural change.

III

Alabados of New Mexico

La Crucifixión de Cristo *(The Crucifixion). Oil painting by Ray John de Aragón.*

Alabados of New Mexico

New Mexico's Penitente alabados vary from one geographic region to another, but they are all emotional expressions of profound religious faith. Although one of their main functions is to unify the various elements of the Penitente rituals, at the same time they provide deep insight into the complex psychology of the members of the Brotherhood. They also should be considered an integral part of the Hispanic culture of the region, and their study could change current views regarding the social and religious life of its Spanish-speaking people.

The alabados are filled with important and irreplaceable information. For example, the hymn *¡Ay! Mi Corazón Amante* (Alas! My Loving Heart) contains a set of rules that all of the members of the Brotherhood must abide by:

Ama a Dios con toda tu alma,
guarda tu respectiva ley,
para pasar a la gloria
esto nos conviene hacer.

Love your God with all of your soul,
Safeguard your respective law,
So you may enter heaven;
This is what we should do.

29

Al hambriento, y a la viuda,	To the hungry and the widow,
al húerfano dale pan,	To the orphan bread dispense,
al sediento un vaso de agua,	To the thirsty a glass of water,
al desnudo vestidura.	To the naked clothes disperse.
32	32
Al cautivo redimir,	To the captive give deliberation,
al enfermo visitar,	To the sick make a visit,
al afligido consuelo,	To the afflicted consolation,
a los muertos enterrar.	And be certain to bury the dead.
33	33

These responsibilities, which were set down in the form of verse, graphically illustrate the fact that the Brothers were dedicated to the service of their fellow human beings. The Brotherhood was a charitable association consecrated to the Passion of Jesus Christ. The Penitentes, as well as the Carmelitas, were under strict obedience to provide help to the poor and upon becoming members actually took a vow of mercy.

The alabados were written down in *cuadernos* (small memoranda or notebooks) by Los Hermanos de la Luz, Brothers of Light. *Cuaderno* (from *cuatro*, meaning four) has been used since the fourteenth century to refer to a small book of sewn pages containing handwritten *ordenanzas* (methodologies), instructions, and notes. In New Mexico, the cuadernos served as guides for devotion and contained instructions outlining the way the Brothers were to comport themselves. Like some of the ancient cuadernos and handwritten books of the Old World, the New Mexican cuadernos were sometimes embellished with drawings of crosses, designs, or illuminated lettering in the margins or at the beginning of poems.

It was the Rezador's responsibility to lead the other Brothers in prayer and devotion. It was also his duty to copy, learn, and teach the alabados to his brethren; this was a tradition that had been handed down for countless generations. None of the ancient cuadernos are extant because as soon as the older copies were too worn and fragile, fresh copies were made and the older ones destroyed.

A careful analysis of the existing cuadernos reveals that the hymns they contain are divided into several types: alabados (in New Mexico, these are sorrowful hymns about the Passion of Christ and his mournful mother), *cánticos* (canticles addressed to the holy infant of Atocha, about Christ's birth), *salves* (salutations or prayers addressed to Mary), *gozos* (verses in praise of Mary but primarily addressed to the saints; in these verses certain words are repeated at the end of every couplet); and *albas* (in New Mexico, these are prayers of thanks intoned at the beginning of a new day). The majority of the hymns in the Penitente cuadernos are alabados (or *alabanzas*), whereas, in the Carmelita cuadernos, salves (hymns to Mary) are more prevalent.

Both the Penitentes and Carmelitas used their cuadernos to maintain their religious faith and also to educate the people. In areas where schools were sparse or nonexistent, many Hispanics learned to read and write by studying the cuadernos. In a few alabados, some of the stanzas curiously end with the word *oi* (I heard); the Penitentes and their families obviously also listened and learned.

The alabados and the other types of religious hymns, coupled with holy images, nurtured the Catholic faith in

New Mexico. The hymns undoubtedly influenced the creative work of the santeros. They not only have high literary value but are also melodic and pleasing to read.

Virtually no effort has been made by previous scholars to cite the composers of the hymns that are distinctly New Mexican in style or content. Among such composers were José A. Gonzáles and Benito Vigil from Pecos, New Mexico, and José María García from Trujillo, New Mexico. By reviewing their versions and styles, it can be determined with some degree of certainty that a few of the hymns were their own compositions; most, however, were of ancient origin and merely recorded by them.

Early collections of Penitente alabados are extremely rare, and most of these have missing pages or are partially illegible. Fortunately, a nearly complete and legible handwritten cuaderno dating to about 1870 has surfaced. Referred to as the Pecos Cuaderno after the area it comes from, it was written by José A. Gonzáles. Significant parts are herein transcribed and translated into English (the translations, as is to be expected, lose some of the flavor of the original versions).

✟ 1 ✟

Mi Alma Vaya Consagrada
May My Soul Travel Consecrated

Mi Alma Vaya Consagrada is the alabado the Brothers sang upon entering their morada, and it served to initiate their penitential rites. The Brothers are reminded that they are to dedicate themselves completely to their duties and never to forget the Brotherhood as they travel on their journey of penitence.

Mi alma vaya consagrada, *y mi cuerpo lleve la luz,* *al entrar esta morada,* *de Nuestro Padre Jesús.*	May my soul journey consecrated, And my body carry the light, On entering this dwelling, Of our Father Jesus Christ.
1	1
Al entrar esta morada, *con mi voz alabaré,* *arrodillado y postrado,* *a Jesús me entregaré.*	On entering this dwelling, With my voice I will sing praises, Kneeling and prostrated, To Jesus I will submit.
2	2
Al entrar esta morada, *mi cuerpo no lleve maneja,* *a Jesús me entregaré,* *a cumplir Semana Santa.*	On entering this dwelling, My body will be meek, To Jesus I'll be devoted, To comply with Holy Week.
3	3
Esta es Semana Santa, *que debemos de pasarla,* *si Dios nos concede vida,* *en esta santa morada.*	This is Holy Week, Which we must retrace, If God grants us life, In this holy dwelling place.
4	4

Los advierto a los cofrados,	I advise all of the Brothers,
clemencia, divina luz,	Clemency, divine light,
que no se olvide	That the Brotherhood be not
el cofrado,	forgotten,
de nuestro Padre Jesús.	Of our Father Jesus Christ.
5	5
Ven los viernes alabar,	Come on Fridays to sing praises,
aquí ésta divina luz,	Here is the divine light,
rezando sus oraciónes,	Reciting the orations,
a nuestro Padre Jesús.	To our Father Jesus Christ.
6	6
De rodillas van los cofrados	On their knees all Brothers travel,
aquí esta la divina luz,	Here is the divine light,
rezando el santo rosario,	Reciting the holy rosary,
de nuestro Padre Jesús.	Of our Father Jesus Christ.
7	7
De rodillas van los	On their knees all Brothers
cofrados,	travel,
llevan un paso tan tierno,	With such sensitive paces,
líbranos Virgen del infierno,	Mary deliver us from Hell,
los que rezan tu rosario.	All of us who recite your rosary.
8	8

✞ 2 ✞

Dios Toca en Esta Misión
God Knocks at This Mission

This prayer is used as part of the penitential ritual. The penitent, while on his knees before the cross in the morada, is asked to listen to what God has expressed through the Holy Writ. He is reminded that penance is the only way to salvation and is asked to remember all the times he was too busy to listen to God. In the fifth stanza, the penitent is told what Christ did for him, and in the following stanzas, he is asked repeatedly to repent and is reminded of God's mercy. Finally, in the last stanza, the alabado calls to all sinners to come to the morada and "hear the voice."

Dios toca en esta misión	God knocks at this mission
las puertas de tu conciencia,	The doors of your conscience,
penitencia, penitencia,	Do penance, do penance,
si quieres tu salvación.	If you want to be saved.
1	1
Penitencia, penitencia,	Do penance, do penance,
ya no peques, hombre atroz,	Sin no more, atrocious man,
examina tu conciencia,	Examine your conscience,
¡Ven al templo, oye la voz!	Come to the temple, hear the voice!
2	2
Tiempo es de hacer penitencia,	It is time to do your penance,
hombre que estas divertido	You who have strayed away,
al no haberte arrepentido,	Since you have not sought repentance,
examina tu conciencia.	Examine your conscience today.
3	3

Llora ya con llanto tierno
no se cumpla tu sentencia;
antes de caer al infierno:
penitencia, penitencia.

Repent with tearful heart,
Don't fulfill your sentence,
Before falling into Hell,
Do penance, do penance.

4

Mira que un Dios humanado
dirigiéndose así a nos,
diciéndonos disfrazado,
"¡Ya no peques hombre atroz!"

Look to that God made human
While directing himself to us,
In his terrible suffering he said,
"Sin no more atrocious man."

5

Como necio no advertiste,
así peques con violencia,
es buen tiempo todavía,
penitencia, penitencia.

Like a fool you didn't listen,
So you sin without restraint,
Now it's time for you to heed,
Do penance, do penance.

6

¡Llora, llora, penitente,
llora tu culpa perdida,
en lágrimas derretidas,
llora tu culpa, inocente!

Cry, cry, you penitent,
Cry for your misguided fault,
In melting sorrow,
Cry for your guilt, mindless one!

7

Haz un auto verdadero,
reconcíliate con Dios,
hoy te dice un misionero,
"¡Ven al templo, oye la voz!"

Make an act of faith that's true,
Reconcile yourself with God,
Today a missionary tells you,
"Come to the temple, hear the voice!"

8

Homtre tibio y sin talento
ya no peques alevoso,
deja tu divertimiento,
¡Ven al templo,
oye la voz!

You who are indifferent and
without talent,
Sin no more, you traitor,
Leave the wayward life,
Come to the temple, hear the voice!

9

Te pierdes sin esperanza
si sigues pecando atroz,
no continúes la venganza,
¡Ven al templo, oye la voz!

10

Si en el mundo te entretienes,
el tiempo se va veloz,
antes de que te condenes
¡Ven al templo, oye la voz!

11

Ya se me acabó el aliento,
ya me voy al Redentor
y si quieres separarte,
¡Ya no peques, hombre atroz!

12

Ven a mí te estrecharé
en mis brazos ambos dos,
para que no llegues pecando,
¡Ven al templo, oye la voz!

13

Alerta que estás perdido,
haz un examen veloz
y así mal entretenido,
¡Ven al templo, oye
la voz!

14

Llega a la mesa sagrada,
deja la culpa feroz,
venid soltero o casada,
¡Ven al templo, oye la voz!

15

You will be lost without hope
If you continue in your wicked way,
Don't continue in your vengeance,
Come to the temple, hear the voice!

10

If in this world you amuse yourself,
Time will swiftly pass,
So before you condemn yourself,
Come to the temple, hear the voice!

11

My vigor has run out,
I'm on my way to the Redeemer
And if you want to pull away,
Sin no more, atrocious man!

12

Come to me and I'll embrace you,
In my arms we'll both rejoice,
So you won't arrive in sin,
Come to the temple, hear the voice!

13

Beware, you could be lost,
Examine your conscience quickly,
And in that way wrongly
entertained,
Come to the temple, hear the voice!

14

Come to the sacred altar,
Leave behind your cruel sin,
Whether single or whether married,
Come to the temple, hear the voice!

15

Entonces necio imagina
que dirás ante mi Dios,
ésta es mi santa doctrina,
¡Ven al templo, oye la voz!

16

Vuelve a mi Dios humanado,
al evangelico de Dios,
al pecador exaltado,
¡Ven al templo, oye la voz!

17

Then, ignorant one, imagine
What you will say before my God,
This is my divine doctrine,
Come to the temple, hear the voice!

16

Return to the God made human,
To the gospel of the Lord,
To all disconcerted sinners,
Come to the temple, hear the voice!

17

✝ 3 ✝

VEN PECODAR Y VERÁS
COME, SINNER, AND YOU WILL SEE

The following alabado is a combination ballad and prayer. It is a long poetic narrative, written in octosyllabic quatrains, of scenes from the Passion. The account is similar to that given by St. Luke in the New Testament. In the first quatrain, the reciter asks to be heard as he relates the story about a man who has been crucified. He portrays Jesus as the Savior of mankind and intersperses heartrending dialogue. At the conclusion, after describing all of the sufferings of Jesus, the reciter alludes to the ascent of Jesus into heaven.

Ven, pecador, y verás *un Señor crucificado,* *padeciendo por el hombre* *y tan cruelmente azotado.*	Come, sinner, and you will see A man who died, Suffering pain for mankind Scourged and crucified.
1	1
En la mesa estaba Cristo *de los doce acompañado* *y con tierna voz decía:* *"Hoy voy ser entregado."*	Christ was at the table, His twelve Apostles attended, And gently he said to them, "Today I will be deserted."
2	2
Con humilde devoción *tomó su divino cuerpo* *y les dió a beber su* *sangre* *que es el Nuevo* *Testamento.*	Enveloped in humble devotion, To them his divine body he bestowed, And gave them his blood to drink, And thus the New Testament was disclosed.
3	3

Les dice a sus escogidos
Cristo, Nuestro Redentor,
"Velad y ver, hijos míos,
que no les tenta el traidor."

He said to those he had chosen,
Christ, our attentive Redeemer,
"My sons, watch and bear with me,
Lest you fall like the betrayer."

4

Y ven venir al traidor,
quien a Jesús fue entregado,
y al instante salió Cristo
y le dice: "A quién buscáis?"

And they see the traitor coming,
The one who had delivered Jesus,
At that instant Christ went forth,
"Whom do you seek?" he inquired.

5

Ellos, con voces muy tiernas
a quien le respondieron:
"No más venimos a buscar
a Jesús de Nazareno."

They, with voices meek,
Responded to him,
"We only come to seek
Jesus of Nazareth."

6

Jesús les dice: "Yo soy,"
y les volvio a publicar
y ellos cayeron en tierra
sin poderse levantar.

Jesus replies, "I am he,"
And again he made himself known,
And they all fell to the ground,
Not being able to stand.

7

Segunda vez les pregunta
con un amor verdadero:
"¿A quién buscáis, inhumanos,
que vienen con atropello?"

And again Jesus asks them,
With a sweet and loving voice of devotion,
"Oh, cruel ones, whom do you seek,
Since you come with such commotion?"

8

Viniendo a Cristo *(Coming to Christ). Nineteenth-century engraving. De Aragón family collection.*

Ellos dicen: "¡A Jesús!"
en tierra vuelven a caerse.
Sólo de ver al Criador,
no podían
levantarse.

"We seek Jesus!" they reply,
To the earth falling bound,
At merely seeing our Lord,
They couldn't get up off the
ground.

9

Jesús dice a los
judíos:
"¡Ay, desdichadas
criaturas
que a Cristo van a
entregar
para cumplir la escritura!"

Jesus says to the men who
betrayed him:
"Oh, you most unfortunate of
creatures,
Christ you will turn over
To comply with the Holy
Scriptures."

10

Ya se arrima el batallón
y Judas con mal intento,
y le dice a Jesucristo:
"¡Dios te guarde, dulce
maestro!"

The battalion finally arrives,
And Judas with bad intention
Said to the Lord Jesus Christ,
"Sweet teacher, may God be your
salvation!"

11

¡Que corazón de criaturas
que con beso de traición
entriegan a los farieseos
este divino Señor!

"What a cruel heart you have
To betray me with a kiss
And turn me over to the Pharisees,
Your Divine Lord, like this!"

12

Llegan estos inhumanos
para volver a prender,
y escupen su dulce rostro
y comienza a padecer.

The inhuman accusers drew near
To take him as their prisoner,
They spit on his loving face,
Then he began to suffer.

13

Ya lo llevan al Calvario
principio de las naciones
dando su rostro Jesús
por aquellos batallones.

14

They conducted him to Calvary,
The kin of all nations,
Hitting the face of Jesus
Was the massing crowd.

14

Dos falsos calumniadores
con terrible voz diciendo,
"¡Que ellos destruyen
un templo
y en tres días fabricarlo!"

15

Two false and wicked accusers
With terrible voices proclaim that
he says,
"If the temple should be destroyed
Then he will rebuild it in three days!"

15

No respondiendo Jesús
ni tan sólo una palabra,
los falsos calumniadores
mal cabaña levantaron.

16

Jesus, our Lord, did not answer,
Gave not a single explanation,
The malicious slanderers continued
To make more accusations.

16

El pontífice le dice:
"¿En nombre de Dios divino,
eres Tú el Hijo de Dios
verdadero
Cristo, rey de los judíos?"

17

The high priest then said,
"In God's divine name are you
The true Son of God,
Christ, King of the
Jews?"

17

Jesús dice a los judíos:
"Yo soy el Dios verdadero
y verás mi majestad
sobre las nubes del cielo."

18

Jesus replied to the Jews,
"I, Son of God, am given
My Kingdom, not on earth but
Above the clouds in Heaven."

18

Con una voz muy porfiada,
le levantan a mi amado
de que había de morir
el que había blasfemado.

With a voice full of hatred,
They falsely accuse him of deception
And condemn him to death
For his blasphemous oration.

19

Mas viendo Jesús a Pedro,
que tres veces lo ha negado,
y le da una mirada,
al Padre Eterno le amó.

19

But Jesus turned to look at Peter,
Who three times has rejected him,
and Peter cast a glance on Jesus,
The Eternal Father who loves him.

20

Al punto ya cantó el gallo
y Pedro empezó a llorar,
lágrimas de contrición
las lloraba sin cesar.

20

At that point, the cock crowed
And Peter began weeping
Tears of contrition
And continued without ceasing.

21

"¡Pequé, mi Jesús, pequé!
¡Pésame el haber negado
tres veces a mi Criador
antes de cantar el gallo!"

21

"I've sinned, my Jesus, I've sinned,
Forgive me for having denied you,
My Creator, three times
Before the cock crew!"

22

Después de tantos martirios
que le dio aquel pueblo ingrato,
por las calles de pasiones
hasta casa de Pilatos.

22

After suffering so much
From the unwavering avengers,
Through the streets of his passion
To the place of Pilate's shelter.

23

Judas, que lo había vendido,
viendo a Jesús
sentenciado,
arrepentido volvió
el dinero que le habian dado.

23

Judas, he who had betrayed him,
After hearing the sentence
pronounced,
Repenting his act returned
The money he had been awarded.

24

24

Judas contra el cielo ha pecado
y desgraciado vendió
la sangre de mi Señor
de Jesús sacramentado.

25

Sólo de ver las afrentas
mofean a mi Jesús,
dician los fariseos:
"¡Muera, muera en una cruz!"

26

Una corona furiosa
con tan terribles espinas
que ricibió en la cabeza
y en esas sienes divinas.

27

Lo conducen al Calvario,
descalzo y con el madero;
tres veces ha caído en tierra,
y le traen un cerineo.

28

Así paga el mundo tan mal
y si murió crucificado.
Que cuando llegó al
Calvario
el aliento le faltó.

29

Una cruel soga le echaron
cuando empezo a padecer
y limpiando el sudor
una piadosa mujer.

30

Judas against heaven has sinned
And has ungratefully shed
The blood of my Savior,
Jesus, the most blessed sacrament.

25

After witnessing the insults,
Mocking my sweet Jesus,
The Pharisees cried,
"Die, die on a cross!"

26

A crown so fierce,
With such terrible thorns,
Was placed on his head
And most divine temples.

27

Shown the way to Calvary,
Barefoot and carrying a cross;
Three times he has fallen,
So they bring him a Cyrenian.

28

The world is so unjust,
And he did die by crucifixion.
And when he reached Calvary,
His spirit was lacking due to
exhaustion.

29

They tied him with a cruel rope
As his sufferings began,
And his sweat was wiped
By a pious woman.

30

Ya la sentencia está dada
por un falso emperador,
el presidente, Pilatos,
"¡Muera, muera el Redentor!"

The sentence has been pronounced
By a faithless emperor,
The judge Pilate,
"Death, death to your Redeemer!"

31

Ya vienen los fariseos
a darle hiel y vinagre,
y ves a mi Redentor
aclamar a su Eterno Padre.

There they come, the Pharisees,
To give him gall and vinegar,
And then our Divine Redeemer
Called on his Heavenly Father.

32

El sol ya se ha obscurecido,
ya no ilumina su luz,
el mundo se ha
conmovido,
viendo morir a
Jesús.

The sun has faded
And the light is lost in darkness,
The earth itself shook and
trembled,
As the death of Jesus was
witnessed.

33

El velo se abrio en
tres partes
las piedras se han dividido.
Y la luna y las estrellas
todas ya se han conmovido.

The veil in the temple was torn
in three
And the stones were divided.
The moon and the stars above,
All were set into motion.

34

Tiembla tres veces la tierra
de ver a Jesús pendiente
de verlo en aguella cruz
y el hombre no se arrepiente.

Three times the earth quaked,
On seeing Jesus suspended,
Seeing him on that cross,
And still man has not repented.

35

Llega María Magdalena,
dando clamores
al cielo
y le dice a Jesucristo:
"¿Hasta Cuando,
Dios Eterno?"

36

Dos varones lo bajaron,
se lo entriegan a María.
Con tierno llanto
le dice:
"¡Ay, Jesús del alma mía!"

37

Lo agarra en sus dulces
brazos,
bañada de compasión;
su dulce rostro le valga
traspasada de dolor.

38

Un dolor tan penetrado
que sintió su corazón
de ver morir a Cristo
en su sagrada pasión.

39

"¡Adiós, adiós,
Jesús mío!
Adíos del cielo y la tierra,
que moriste por el hombre
en una cruz verdadera!"

40

Mary Magdalene arrived,
Lamenting with bitter tears to
heaven,
And to Jesus Christ she said,
"My Eternal God, when will
I see you?"

36

Two men lowered him
from the cross,
And delivered him to Mary.
Weeping softly she said,
"Oh Jesus of my heart!"

37

And she took him in her loving
arms,
Weeping with compassion,
That his beautiful face may
Transcend its affliction.

38

A pain so penetrating
Felt deep with compassion
Upon seeing her loving son die
In his most sacred passion.

39

"Farewell, farewell, my loving
Jesus!
Farewell, from this earthly place,
You who died for all mankind
On the one true cross!"

40

Fué enterrado en un sepulcro,
el cual José le donó,
así mismo la mortaja,
la que su madre le dío.

41

Después de tantos martirios,
al sepulcro fué María,
pero hallándolo tapado,
con aguello gozaría.

42

Abajó un ángel del
cielo
y la piedra removió
y diciéndole a María:
"Ya Cristo resucitó."

43

He was buried in a sepulcher
That Joseph contributed,
As was also the shroud
Which his mother presented.

41

After so much suffering
Mary visited the tomb,
But finding it closed and sealed,
She put her trust in God.

42

An angel came down from
heaven,
And the stone he removed,
And thereupon said to Mary,
"Christ is resurrected."

43

✞ 4 ✞

Contempla Alma y Considera
Contemplate and Consider

In this hymn, the sinner is asked to contemplate the Passion and is reminded of the importance of repenting his sins. If the remorseful penitent agrees to partake of the Passion, then he is told he may join with the Savior in carrying the heavy cross. If he does not learn through Christ's example and his own penitential exercises, then the sinner is told he can expect nothing more than the eternal fires of Hell. But if the penitent prostrates himself before the merciful and divine judge and begs forgiveness, and if he receives communion, then the gates of Heaven will open for him.

Contempla, alma, y considera	Contemplate and consider
en la divina pasión	The divine Passion
de aquel divino Cordero,	Of that divine shepherd,
Cristo Dios, nuestro Señor.	Christ Jesus, our Redeemer.
1	1
Anda, ingrato y cruel traidor,	Come ungrateful and cruel traitor,
el día se ha de llegar,	Your day is coming near,
y de esto cuenta has de dar	Think about this, heed and listen,
este divino Señor.	This our Divine Savior.
2	2
Considera en su pasión,	Consider his Passion,
que es el tesoro más grande,	Which is the largest treasure,
allí derramó su sangre	He shed his blood for all of us,
este divino Señor.	This our Divine Savior.
3	3

Si quieres acompañar
aquella divina luz,
con las caídas que va dando
con el peso de la cruz.

If you really want to follow
That divine light,
Then fall as he once fell,
Under the burden of the cross.

4

Le dice a su eterno Padre
la hora es llegada ya.
"Has de beber este cáliz,
que se haga tu voluntad."

He told his heavenly Father
The hour had finally come,
"I must take this golden chalice,
Let your will, not mine, be done."

5

Míralo con tanto amor
al divino Redentor,
que por tres veces fue
al huerto
y postrado hizo oración.

Look at the Divine Redeemer,
Who is filled with so much love,
Three times he went to the garden
Kneeling he prayed to our Father
above.

6

Si no aprendes la lección,
ni contemplas tu ejercicio,
mira que el día del juicio
espera un grán temor.

If you don't learn this lesson
And do your penitence here,
Then the final day of judgment
You must await in dreadful fear.

7

"¡Válgame Dios! ¿Qué haré yo?"
dirás cuando estés boqueando,
cuando Dios te esté llamando,
cuenta con tanto rigor.

"Oh my God, what shall I do?"
You will say on your dying day,
As you go to meet God face to face,
In convulsive shuddering all the way.

8

¿Qué harás allí, pecador,
viendo al justo juez sagrado,
leyéndole la sentencia,
que te apartes de su lado?

What will you do then, sinner,
The just judge full of grace,
Reading you your sentence,
You must leave in disgrace?

9

¿Qué tormentos te darán
en aquel fuego metido,
quemándote las entrañas,
abrazado y consumido?

What torments will they give you,
In that infinite fire of Hell,
Your insides enflamed,
Burning and emaciated.

10

Considera, alma perdida,
mira, no vayas allá,
que es una pena crecida
por toda la eternidad.

Please consider, you lost soul,
Look, don't go there,
For it is a terrible penalty,
And a heavy price to bear.

11

Arrepiéntate, cristiano,
con todo tu corazón,
y deja este mal estado
y busca a tu Redentor.

Repent, O Christian brother,
With all of your heart,
Turn away from sin altogether,
And find your Redeemer.

12

Si quieres tener perdón,
recibe un grande consuelo,
humíllate al confesor
que allí hallarás tu remedio.

If you want to have your pardon
And receive your consolation,
Kneel before your prime confessor
To receive your reparation.

13

Si te echan la bendición,
levántate, sin recelo;
si quieres subir al cielo,
recibe la comunión.

If you are given a benediction,
Get up, without suspicion,
If you want to reach Heaven,
Receive Holy Communion.

14

Pero te advierto y te digo
que si subes al altar,
has de ir bien arrepentido
y sin pecado mortal.

But I advise you and I say,
If you go up to receive communion,
You should go with a feeling of repentance
And without sin or face damnation.

15

Monte Calvario *(Penitente Mount Calvary). El Cerro, New Mexico. Photograph by Lucía de Aragón.*

✝ 5 ✝

AY! MI CORAZÓN AMANTE
ALAS! MY LOVING HEART

This alabado suggests that the Nazarene brother should do penance lest he show his ungratefulness to the Savior. It then goes on to relate the suffering of the Lord in his Passion. From stanza 28 to stanza 36, all the duties of the members are listed. For example, in stanza 32 the brothers are told to feed the hungry, to give drink to the thirsty, and to clothe the naked, and in stanza 33 they are told to visit the sick, console the afflicted, and bury the dead. In the final stanzas, the penitent promises to occupy his time with doing good deeds for the greater glory of Jesus the Nazarene.

¡Ay! mi corazón amante,
Nazareno penitente,
sube a la cumbre eminente,
con dolor más penetrante.

Alas! my loving heart,
Nazarene penitent,
Reach the eminent summit,
With penetrating pain.

1

Triste pecador advierte
con qué pecado has vivido
y si no haces penitencia,
serás desagradecido.

1

Mournful sinner be aware
Of the sins which you carry,
And if you do not repent,
You are very ungrateful.

2

De sus sienes tan heridas
con esos juncos marinos,
brotando gotas de sangre
por mí tan desconocido.

2

From your temples wounded
By these spiny thorns,
The drops of blood rush forward
For one who is a stranger.

3

3

Su dulce cabello estaba
en sangre y polvo teñido,
todo ha sido por mi causa
y mi corazón tan frío.

Your sweet hair was covered,
With blood and dirt entangled,
All for my sake,
And my cold, cold heart.

4

Sus mejillas tan golpeadas,
de aquellos crueles sayones,
no fueron más que tus culpas,
que ni sientes pero ni oyes.

His cheeks bruised and injured,
By those cruel executioners,
For no more than my weaknesses,
While your senses remain dormant.

5

Mira sus labios con sangre
por tanto que te estimaba
por hablarte con amor
al tormento se entregaba.

Look at his bloody lips,
Because he loved you so,
Because he spoke to you with love,
In torment he had to go.

6

Su hermosa barba partida,
de las crueles bofetadas,
cómo sufre con dureza,
tanto martirio en su cara.

His most precious beard parted,
With such cruel aggression,
Oh the suffering he endures,
So much torment on his face.

7

Su garganta adormecida
de la soga que le echaron
y tú durmiendo en pecado
por que mi Jesús orara.

His throat benumbed
From the rope which they pulled,
And you sleeping in sin
While my Jesus prays for you.

8

Sus hombros todos llagados,
los pedazos le faltaron,
y a ti te faltó la enmienda,
por el pecado en que estaba.

His shoulders wounded,
With flesh torn away,
And you lacking in reparation,
For your sinfulness.

9

Sus brazos tan fatigados,
de la cuerda que le echaron,
y tu pobre alma manchada,
en la vida que le dabas.

10

Sus espaldas amoratadas
prietas de azotes que daban,
que brotaban fuertes lagos
de esa sangre inmaculada.

11

Su dulce costado abierto,
que hasta el corazón hirió,
manos con gotas de sangre,
que todo el mundo conocío.

12

Sus manos agujereadas,
cuyo clavos remacharon
y tu traspasada vida,
en delitos transformada.

13

Con cordeles corredizos
sus dulces piernas ligaron,
que traspadada la carne,
hasta el hueso le llegaron.

14

En las rodillas corriendo sangre,
de tanto que lo ultrajaron,
de golpes y bofetadas,
que el peso a caer lo agobiaba.

15

His arms suffered from exhaustion,
From the rope of encumbrance,
And your poor soul an indication
Of your life far from deliverance.

10

His torso full of contusions,
Blackened by the lashes,
His wounds creating lakes
Of his most immaculate blood.

11

His sweet side was pierced,
Even until his heart was injured,
Hands with blood afflicted,
That all of the world witnessed.

12

His pierced hands,
In which nails were secured,
And your afflicted life,
In which your crime was
transformed.

13

With binding cords
His sweet legs were joined,
Which cut through his flesh,
Even reaching to the bone.

14

From his knees blood ran,
He was so outrageously treated,
From the hitting and the blows,
With the weight his body fell down.

15

Grillos de hierro tenían
los pies atados del rey,
que impusieron los Judíos,
también impuesto a su ley.

16

Sus santos pies delicados,
que la carne le brotó,
así has de hacer penitencia,
por el alma que Dios te dio.

17

Con duros clavos de hierro,
que en sus pies le clavaron,
por tu deuda pecador,
tanta sangre has derramado.

18

Cuando habrán desfallecido,
sus fuerzas descoyuntadas,
traerán a un Cirineo,
que el madero levantará.

19

Caminaba a paso tierno,
porque fuerza no tenia,
sus ojos estaban inertes,
por la congoja y fatiga.

20

Y así caía muchas veces
por la crueldad con
que lo veían
sin poderse levantar
los tormentos lo rendían.

21

Shackles of iron were set
On the feet of our good king,
Which were imposed by the Jews,
In compliance with their law.

16

His holy feet so delicate,
With the flesh that was torn,
This is how you should do penance,
For the life God has given you.

17

Hardened nails of iron,
Into his feet were placed,
For your sinful indebtedness,
So much blood you have spilled.

18

When you have grown faint,
Your strength will not endure,
They will bring a Cyrenian,
And your cross he will secure.

19

He walked very lightly,
For his strength was all but gone,
His eyes were glazed from anguish,
And nothing could be done.

20

And thus he fell so many
times,
They saw him with disdain,
At times he couldn't rise again,
In torture and restraint.

21

Con todos estos martirios
llegó Jesús a expirar,
atado de pies y manos,
en la cruz hoy lo verás.

22

Las palabras que Jesús habló,
al tiempo de ir a expirar,
"Sed tengo," dijo en la cruz,
para poder expirar.

23

Ya va José y Nicodemos
y lo bajan de la cruz
y lo llevan al sepulcro,
en un paño a Jesús.

24

Y cuando resucitó Jesús
al cielo ardiente,
lo presentan a Dios Padre,
su cuerpo hecho penitente.

25

Tiembla el Justo y siente el
alma,
al ver el cargo que os hace,
por esa sangre preciosa,
que tu Redentor traspasa.

26

Si me tienes compasión
que justamente ha de ser,
por mis culpas el perdón,
pues te conviene el hacer.

27

With all these great sufferings,
Our Savior neared expiration,
With his hands and feet bound,
Today you will see his crucifixion.

22

The words which Jesus uttered
At the time before he expired,
"I'm thirsty," he proclaimed,
Because he was so tired.

23

There go Joseph and Nicodemus
To lower him from the cross
And take him to the sepulcher,
In the shroud they carry Jesus.

24

And when Jesus was resurrected,
To his passionate Heaven,
They presented him to his Father,
With his body made penitent.

25

The Just One shakes and my
heart breaks,
To see what we have done,
For that precious blood,
That our Redeemer shed.

26

If you have compassion,
As so justly ought to be,
My faults will be forgiven,
For he has agreed to do this for me.

27

Si no haces confesión,
que justamente ha de ser,
se ha de llegar la ocasión,
que te has de condenar.

28

If your sins you don't confess,
As so justly ought to be,
Then the occasion will arise
When your condemnation you
will see.

28

Ama a Dios con toda tu alma,
guarda y respeta su ley,
para pasar a la gloria
esto nos conviene hacer.

29

Love your God with all your soul,
Safeguard and respect his law,
So you may enter heaven,
This is what we have to do.

29

En el mundo considera,
al huérfano has de ver,
socorre al necesitado,
recompensa has de tener.

30

Here on Earth you must consider,
To seek the orphan,
Help all of those in need,
Recompense you will receive.

30

La esperanza en el Señor,
que por nosotros murió,
y con una fe sin tasa,
la has de ver por que te honró.

31

Your hope in our dear Savior
Exists because he died for us,
And with a faith unbounding,
You'll learn of his just cause.

31

Al hambriento, y a la viuda,
al huérfano déle pan,
al sediento un vaso de agua,
al desnudo vestidura.

32

To the hungry and the widow,
To the orphan bread dispense,
To the thirsty a glass of water,
To the naked clothes disperse.

32

Al cautivo redimir,
al enfermo visitar,
al afligido consuelo,
a los muertos enterrar.

33

To the captive give liberation,
To the sick make a visit,
To the afflicted give consolation,
And be certain to bury the dead.

33

Llora contrito tu culpa,
confiesa a tu Redentor,
cómo hizo Magdalena,
y al punto hubo
remisión.

Cry to your Redeemer,
Confess your sins in contrition,
Just as Mary Magdalene has done
And was rewarded with
exculpation.

34

Mira esa misericordia,
que te promete el perdón,
si a tu prójimo
bien amas,
pues es la mayor razón.

Just think of the sacredness,
When forgiveness will be given,
If you love your fellowman with
kindness,
This is your main reason.

35

Mira que hay Dios de piedad
y con poder infinito,
perdona con caridad,
al que le busca contrito.

There is a God of mercy,
With power never ending,
Who kindly forgives everyone
Who seeks him penitent.

36

Soy la obra de tus manos,
hoy mi Jesús Nazareno,
dame un corazón contrito,
paraque siempre obre lo bueno.

I was fashioned by your hands,
Today, please my Lord,
Give me a contrite heart,
So that I'll always seek good.

37

A tu divina presencia,
mis pasos encaminar,
por una preciosa senda,
que siempre te ha de agradar.

To your divine presence
Guide my footsteps,
In that most precious path
Which will always please me.

38

En fin recibe mis voces
con lágrimas de mis ojos,
que puedan así agradarte,
y quitarte los enojos.

Finally, hear my voice
With tears in my eyes,
So that I may always please you
And never bring you sighs.

39

La Penitencia *(The Penitence). Nineteenth-century engraving. De Aragón family collection.*

✝ 6 ✝

Jesus de Mi Corazón
Jesus of My Heart

In this touching appeal for the Savior's mercy, the remorseful sinner confesses his sinfulness and promises to mend his ways. He admits he has consistently offended the Lord and then goes on to relate the Savior's bodily and mental anguish. The penitent ends with a final verse about the true loving kindness of his lord and master.

Jesús de mi corazón
justo juez, mi Padre amado,
aquí me tienes postrado,
implorando tu perdón.

Jesus of my heart,
Fair judge and loving Father,
Here I am at your feet,
forever imploring your pardon.

1

Soy el más vil pecador,
tus leyes he quebrantado,
y pues contra ti he pecado,
misericordia Señor.

I am the most vile sinner,
A transgressor against the law,
And against you I have sinned,
Compassionate Savior.

2

Yo he dejado de serviros,
mil veces os he
agobiado,
escúchame Padre amado,
oye mi llanto y suspiros.

I have failed to serve,
A thousand times I have been
belligerent,
O, loving Father continue hearing
My cries and my lament.

3

Pésame de corazón,
Jesús haberte ofendido,
Dios santo ten compasión,
del que tan ingrato ha sido.

For forgiveness my heart is aspiring,
Jesus, I have offended you so,
Holy Father show compassion,
Although I have been so ungrateful.

4

¡Oh, dulce Jesús de mi vida!
santo fuerte omnipotente,
he aquí la oveja perdida,
que a voz llega reverente.

4

O, sweet Jesus of my life!
Powerful God, omnipotent,
I am a lost sheep,
I kneel before you to repent.

5

Bien sé que no merecía,
alcanzar de ti el perdón,
dámelo, ¡Oh Dios! por María,
por tu sagrada pasión.

5

I know full well that I'm not worthy
To ask you your holy pardon,
Please give it to me, Lord, for Mary
And for your holy, holy passion.

6

Por el copioso sudor,
que en el huerto derramaste,
por el cáliz que apuraste,
misericordia Señor.

6

For your abundant agony,
Which in the garden you suffered,
For the chalice that you purified,
Merciful Savior.

7

Por los pasos que tu diste,
llevando a cuestas la cruz,
y por las caídas que hiciste,
misericordia Señor.

7

For the footsteps that you took,
Carrying the cross on your back,
And for the many times you fell,
Merciful Savior.

8

Por el santísimo velo en
que fue tu rostro estampado,
salva Señor este suelo,
y líbralo del pecado.

8

For the holy veil on which
Your holy image was imprinted,
Save this world, my Lord, my God,
And deliver it from sin.

9

9

Por la terrible violencia,
con que fuiste desnudado,
misericordia y clemencia,
Jesucristo, Padre amado.

10

En fin Señor por la cruz,
en la que fuiste enclavado,
perdóname buen Jesús,
y líbrame del
pecado.

11

Por la bofetada atroz,
que sufriste humildemente,
perdóname Dios clemente,
misericordia Señor.

12

Por la corona bunzante
que os pusieron con crueldad,
perdóname padre amante,
ten de nosotros piedad.

13

Echame tu bendición,
justo juez, Padre amoroso,
para alcanzar el reposo,
en tu mansión celestial.

14

Jesuscristo aplaca tu ira,
tu justicia y tu rigor,
y por tu preciosa sangre,
misericordia Señor.

15

For the terrible violence,
With which you were disrobed,
I beg your mercy and compassion,
Jesus Christ, loving Father.

10

Finally, Lord, for the cross
On which you were crucified,
Forgive me, Lord Jesus,
And liberate me, for whom you
died.

11

For the many, many blows
That you suffered in submission,
Forgive me, oh clement Jesus,
Merciful Father.

12

For the pointed crown
Which was placed with cruelty,
Pardon me, loving Father,
Have pity on us.

13

Bestow on me your benediction,
Fair judge and loving Father,
So that I may reach glorification
In your most celestial mansion.

14

Dear Christ, appease your ire,
Your justice, and your harshness,
And for your precious blood,
Lord, give your loving kindness.

15

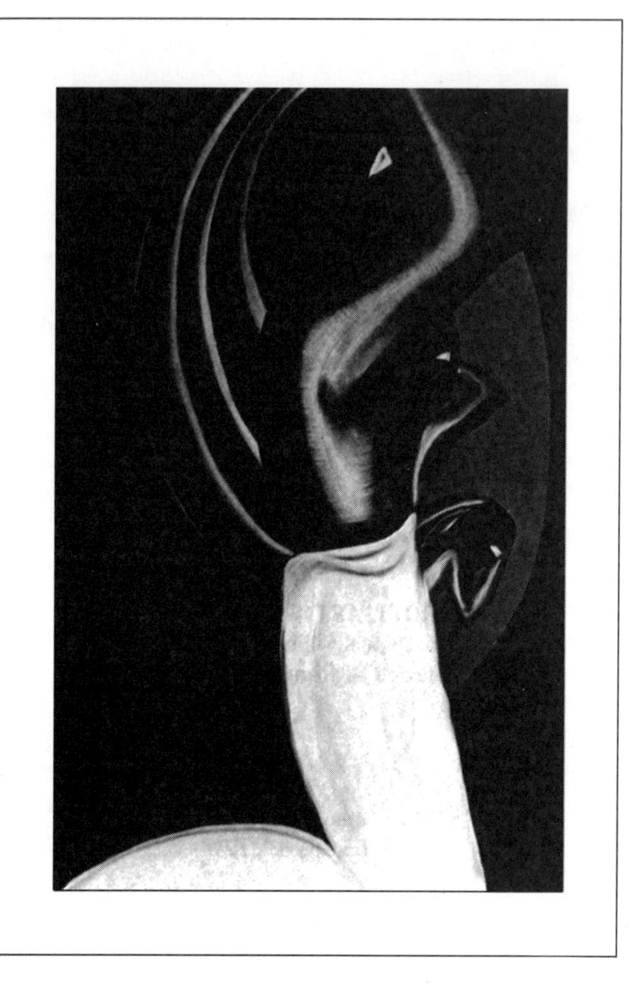

Los Penitentes, *oil painting on canvas, by Ray John de Aragón.*

✝ 7 ✝

Por la Calle Mas Amarga
By the Most Painful Road

In this traditional Penitente religious ballad, the singer passionately implores the Savior to forgive his sins.

Por la calle mas amarga	By the most painful road
pasearon a mi Jesús,	Our Lord was taken,
le leyeron su sentencia,	They gave him his sentence
lo clavaron en la cruz.	And nailed him to the cross.
1	1
Ya vienen los fariseos	And there come the Pharisees
a cometir el pecado	To commit their sin,
en busca de mi Jesús,	In search of Jesus,
un Señor sacramentado.	Our anointed king.
2	2
Ya vienen los fariseos	The Pharisees in search of our Lord,
con aquel rigor airado,	With arrogance in stride,
le dieron una lanzada	Swung their most brutal sword
en su divino costado.	Into his most divine side.
3	3
Mi Dios por vuestro pecado	My God, due to our sin
es causa de su pasión,	You went through your passion,
de su mucho padecer,	You suffered so much
de mi Dios y Redentor.	My God and my Redeemer.
4	4

Oiganme bien, pecadores:	Hear me well, oh sinners!
hagan buena confesión	Make a good confession,
para que entre en vuestro pecho	So that into your hearts,
este divino Señor.	This divine lord may enter.
5	5
A la justicia divina	Divine justice
aclamarla sin cesar,	We all will soon seek,
que perdone nuestras culpas	Asking for pardon
en la corte celestial.	In the celestial court.
6	6
Con aquel dolor inmenso	With immense pain and sorrow,
como indigno pecador,	Like an unworthy sinner,
perdón de mis grandes culpas	Forgive me my great faults,
yo te pido, gran Señor.	I beg, O great Savior.
7	7
Perdóname mis pecados,	Forgive me my sins,
pues tú sabes cuantos son,	You know which they are,
padre de misericordia,	O merciful Father,
por tu infinita pasión.	For your infinite compassion.
8	8
Ten cuidado de mis culpas,	You are aware of my great weakness,
pues las habrás observado;	As you have observed,
pido perdón a mi Dios	I ask for your forgiveness, Lord,
por lo mucho que he pecado.	For I have greatly sinned.
9	9
Busca un Cristo de la tierra,	Find a disciple of Christ,
semejanza del Señor,	A follower of his example,
para que absuelva nuestras culpas	So that he may absolve me of my sins,
para alcanzar el perdón.	And grant me forgiveness.
10	10

Esta es mi querida madre,
es vuestra madre y señora
madre llena de dolor,
también nuestra intercesora.

11

A este Padre verdadero,
he de aclamar sin cesar,
que es el Padre verdadero
de la corte celestial.

12

He de llevar con presteza,
dentro de mi corazón;
para que absuelva mis culpas,
mi Dios y mi Redentor.

13

Perdóname, Padre Eterno,
por lo mucho que he pecado,
por tu infinita pasión
y la llaga del costado.

14

Tengo una dulce morada
dentro de mi corazón
para que estampes en ella
tu santísima pasión.

15

Vi un amor verdadero
en la vida singular
también un árbol divino
de la corte celestial.

16

This is my beloved mother,
As we should all address her,
Mother filled with pain and sorrow,
Also our great intercessor.

11

To my almighty God and the Father
I should proclaim to the end
That he is the true Redeemer
Of the celestial court.

12

I should carry him in haste,
Within my heart,
So that he may absolve my sins,
My God and my Redeemer.

13

Forgive me, Father of all eternity,
For all that I have sinned,
For your infinite passion,
And your wounded back.

14

I have a sweet lodging
Deep within my heart,
So that you will imprint on it
Your most holy passion.

15

I saw a true love
In a single life
And a divine cross
In the celestial court.

16

¡Ay, Dios y mi amada madre!
¡Madre llena de dolores!
cobíjanos con tu manto
por tu infinita pasión.

17

Pues eres pastor divino,
lo he de aclamar sin cesar,
que perdóne nuestras culpas
en la corte celestial.

18

Oh, dear God and loving mother!
Sweet mother full of pain!
Cover me with the mantle
Of your infinite compassion.

17

You are the divine pastor
And I praise you without end,
You forgive me, my faults,
From the celestial court.

18

✞ 8 ✞

Por el Rastro de la Sangre
Along the Trail of Blood

This alabado, sung to a very sad melody in bass tenor, is one of the most popular of the Penitente hymns. In the past it was always sung from memory, since all of the Brothers were required to learn it. The Brothers sang it during the penitential exercises in the morada and also when walking to their place of calvary while whipping themselves. More importantly, they sang it during the ceremony of Las Tinieblas (Tenebrae service), which consists of matins and lauds sung on the evenings of Thursday, Friday, and Saturday during Holy Week. Until the early 1900s, this alabado was sung not only in the moradas during Holy Week but also in many of the old parochial churches in the smaller villages of New Mexico.

Por el rastro de la sangre consists of quatrains in which the second and fourth lines rhyme. It is found in many regions of the Spanish-speaking world, but this New Mexican version differs considerably from other versions.

Por el rastro de la sangre *que Jesucristo derrama,* *camina la Virgen pura* *en una fresca mañana.*	Along the trail of blood Which Jesus Christ was shedding, Traveled his mother, the Virgin Mary, One cold and chilly morning.
1	1
Como era tan de mañana, *a la hora que caminaba,* *las companas de Belén* *solas tocaban el alba.*	Since the day was just beginning At the hour she was walking, Only the bells of Bethlehem Were ringing in the morning.
2	2

Ya se encuentra con San Juan	She encountered St. John,
y de esta manera le habla:	And this is what she had to say,
"¿No ha pasado por aquí	"Has he not passed by here,
el Hijo de mis entrañas?"	Jesus, my precious son, today?"
3	3
"Por aquí pasó, señora,	"He most certainly did, my dear lady,
antes que el gallo cantara;	Before the cock woke the day;
cinco mil azotes lleva	Five thousand lashes lay
en sus sagradas espaldas.	On his sacred shoulders as he passed this way.
4	4
"Una cruz lleva en sus hombros	"He carried a cross upon his shoulders,
de madera muy pesada;	Of very heavy wood I should say;
tres clavos lleva en sus manos	Three nails he held in his hand,
con los que ha de ser clavado.	Which will be used on him today.
5	5
"Y una corona de espinas,	"He also carried a crown of thorns,
con que ha de ser coronado;	To be used for coronation;
padeciendo por el hombre	Suffering for all mankind,
mi Jesús crucificado.	My dear Jesus, in crucifixion.
6	6
"Soga gruesa en su garganta	"A thick rope around his throat
que los judíos le estiraba,"	The Jews continued pulling,
cada tirón que le daban,	And every pull was so unkind,
mi Jesús se arrodillaba."	On his knees he continued falling.
7	7

"Mi Jesús crucificado,
que por mí estás de esa suerte,
has que me valga
la muerte
la sangre que has derramado.

"My Jesus crucified,
Suffering for me,
I prayed that I may be worthy of
death
For the blood you have shed for me.

8

"La herida de su costado,
sea mi eterna habitación,
válgame ya expiar
su cruz, su muerte y pasión.n"

8

"The wound in his side,
Should be my eternal habitation,
Grant that I may make amends for
His cross, his death, and his passion."

9

Válgame, el Padre
amoroso
en la postrera agonía,
los dolores de María
y martirios de su esposo.

9

Forgive me, my God and beloved
Father,
For your humbling agony,
The pains and sorrows of Mary,
And the suffering of her husband.

10

El que esta pasión cantare
todos los viernes del año
saca un ánima de penas
y la suya del pecado.

10

He who recites this passion,
Every Friday of the year,
Releases a soul from affliction
And prevents sin from coming near.

11

11

Nuestra Señora de los Ángeles *(Our Lady of the Angels), by J. Guadalupe Góngora. Nineteenth-century engraving, Mexico. De Aragón family collection.*

✝ 9 ✝

CONTEMPLEMOS TODOS
EVERYONE BEHOLD

This alabado describes the painful feelings of Mary, the mother of Jesus, as she watches her beloved son whipped and eventually crucified. It contains a few narrative lines in which Mary laments her son's suffering. In stanza 21, Mary appears as the loving mother, mourning over the body of her son, which she holds in her arms.

Contemplemos todos	Everyone behold
esta triste madre	This most sorrowful mother
mirando el sepulcro,	Seeing the tomb
y en la cruz la sangre.	And on the cross his blood.
1	1
Madre afligidísima,	Mother so afflicted,
llena de pesar,	So filled with grief,
siguiendo a vuestro Hijo,	Following her son,
lo van a azotar.	Who will suffer from the whip.
2	2
"¡Qué culpas tan grandes	"Oh, what great guilt
al ver al verdugo,	To see such cruelty,
azotando a mi Hijo	They whip my son
con varas de junco!	With sticks of rush!
3	3
"¡Qué culpas tan grandes	"Oh, what great guilt,
a mi Hijo procuran!	It's my son they procure!
¡Lo van a amarrar	They will bind him
en una columna!"	To a column!"
4	4

Sigue la porfía,
el que da más recio.
La sangre inocente,
le rompen del pecho.

The game continues
To see who hits harder,
The innocent blood
Gushes from his chest.

5

Carne virginal,
azotes cubiertos,
le vacunaron
su santa cabeza.

Virginal flesh,
Covered with welts,
They lacerated
His most holy head.

6

"Con juncos marinos,
vida coronada,
a mi Hijo divino
que tuvo encarnado."

"With aquatic rushes,
His life was crowned,
My divine son
That was made flesh."

7

Más de cinco mil
azotes le han dado
hasta que la fuerza
se le ha acabado.

More than five thousand
Lashes unmercifully given
Until his strength
Can no longer endure.

8

Las que tengan hijos,
voy a convidar,
porque Pilatos
lo va a sentenciar.

Those who have children
Are the ones I invite
Because Pontius Pilate
Will sentence him to die.

9

Seguimos el llanto
para descansar,
la sangre inocente,
no ha de pagar.

We follow the wailing
So that we may rest,
For he who is innocent
Should not be made to pay.

10

Qué dolor tan grande
la madre tenía
de ver a Jesús,
que no se movía.

What unbearable pain
His mother did have
To see her son Jesus,
Who did not move.

11

¡Adiós mi Jesús,
mi Padre amoroso,
muere en una cruz,
por un sedicioso!

11

Goodbye, my dear Jesus,
My sweet loving Father,
Who died on the cross
For one so seditious!

12

Escuchen atentos,
la lamentación,
la pasión y muerte,
de nuestro Señor.

12

Listen attentively
To our lamentation
Over the suffering and death
Of our most precious Jesus.

13

"Adiós, Hijo amado
de mi corazón,
la luz de los cielos
se fue y me dejó."

13

"Goodbye, beloved Son
Of my broken heart,
The light from the heavens
Has left me here alone."

14

Madre mira a tu Hijo
con tantos dolores,
te dejo fiadora
de los pecadores.

14

Mother, you look at your son
With so much grief and pain,
He left you in charge
Of us sinners here below.

15

Huérfanos y viudas
vamos a llorar,
los desempeñados,
vamos a buscar.

15

Orphans and widows,
Let's gather to cry,
The redeemed ones,
We shall seek.

16

16

Al Monte Calvario
me han de acompañar,
a ver la hermosura,
pues que va a expirar.

17

Alzado en la cruz,
mofado de gente,
deseando el no tenerlo,
dentro de su vientre.

18

Al pie de la cruz,
cayó sin sentido,
viendo arriba y al verlo
en tanto martirio.

19

Donde ellas mancebos,
vamos a llorar,
José y Nicodemos,
lo van a bajar.

20

"Lo echan en mis brazos,
aquella criatura
y en mi corazón
fué su sepultura."

21

Se lo quitan luego,
lo echan en el sepulcro,
ponen un sudario,
que le queda al mundo.

22

To Mount Calvary
You all should come,
To see the beauty
Which will transpire.

17

Raised on the cross,
Jeered at and scoffed,
He didn't want to hear
That he was so rebuffed.

18

At the foot of the cross,
She fell down senseless,
Upon seeing the torture
Of her martyred son.

19

We who journey with him
Must gather to cry,
As Joseph and Nicodemus
Lowered him to us.

20

"They put him in my arms,
Child that I bore,
To lay him to rest
In the tomb of my heart."

21

They take him from her quickly,
They lay him in the tomb,
Cover him gently with his holy
shroud,
Which remains here on earth.

22

✝ 10 ✝

DIVIDIDO EL CORAZÓN
DIVIDED IS HER HEART

This hymn begins as a ballad dealing with the Passion of Jesus and ends as a prayer. It introduces Mary as a mother with a broken heart. In stanza 2, Mary says, "Oh, my Son and light of my eyes, You have chosen to die for mankind." Stanzas 3 to 6 depict the Passion and Mary's sorrowful agony. Mary is described as an afflicted turtle dove crying for her son and stating they have not only taken his life but that of his mother's also. Again, Mary speaks directly to her son in stanzas 7 to 9, saying, "I am so lonely, now that you have been taken from me. Where have you gone without me? Oh, Son of my soul, sweetness of my life, where have you gone? I am left without reason to live, Redeemer of the universe, creator of life!" In stanzas 10 to 14, more scenes of the Passion are described, including the scene where Mary, at the foot of the cross, takes Jesus in her arms—a shining example of love. In stanza 15, everyone is invited to share in Mary's sorrow and to cry with her in her solitude. In the final verse, mankind is given reason to hope: "But the gates of heaven were opened for Jesus resurrected, and all the souls who had been waiting he took with him to heaven."

Dividido el corazón,	Divided is her heart,
llora María sin consuelo,	Mary weeps without relief,
la noche pasó en desvelo,	As the night is passed in grief,
contemplando en la pasión.	Meditating on the Passion.
1	1

"¡Ay, Hijo y luz de mis ojos,
ya lo van a
sentenciar!"
Murió clavado en la cruz
que al hombre quiso salvar.

"Oh, Son and light of my eyes,
They're going to pass judgment on
you!"
He died nailed to the cross
For the salvation of mankind.

2

Como tórtola afligida,
gime y llora por su amado,
que faltándole a su lado,
le falta su misma vida.

Like an afflicted dove,
Injured, grieving for her loved one,
Feeling the loss of her son,
Her life is without love now.

3

Pilatos lo sentenció
en su tribunal sentado,
y como hombre desdichado,
lo conducen al Calvario.

Pilate passing judgment,
In his tribunal he was sitting,
And like a wretched man bleeding,
To Mount Calvary he was taken.

4

En amarga soledad,
suspira vuestra paloma
por ver si acaso se asoma
de mi Dios la claridad.

In bitter loneliness,
Our dove is out there sighing,
To see if he approaches
With my God's guiding light.

5

"¡Ay, Hijo de mis entrañas!
Hijo de todo mi amor,
muerta ha quedado tu madre,
dividido el corazón!

"Oh, Son of my dear heart!
Son of all my being,
Without life is your mother,
Divided is my heart!

6

"En una noche tan triste,
mi Dios me ha desamparado,
sola y sin ti me he quedado.
Hijo mió, ¿dónde te fuiste?

"On a night so full of sorrow,
My God left me here forsaken,
You were from me taken.
My Son, where have you gone?

7

"¡Ay, Hijo del alma miá,
dulce encanto de mi vida!
¿Dónde estás, dulce Jesús?
¿Dónde estás, prenda querida?

"Oh, Son of my dear soul,
Sweet enchantment of my life!
Where are you, my sweet Jesus?
Where are you, precious jewel?

8

"¿Para qué quiero la vida
sin mi Hijo, Verbo Encarnado,
Redentor del Universo,
Señor de todo lo creado?

8

"Why should I want life
Without my son, word incarnate,
Redeemer of the universe,
Lord of all creation?

9

"Visten de luto los atros,
que ya mi Hijo va a expirar,
estremézcase la tierra,
ayúdenos a lamentar."

9

"The stars are dressed in mourning,
For my son will soon depart,
The earth will shake and tremble,
Help us cry when it does start."

10

Lo conducen al Calvario
con el sello de Jesús,
le clavan sus santas manos
en los brazos de la cruz.

10

They take him on to Calvary,
With the seal of Christ the King,
They nail his holy hands,
To the arms of the cross.

11

Alma de Jesús divina,
de su cuerpo se apartó,
cuando subió al cielo,
empero,
en cuerpo y alma subió.

11

The spirit of our divine Jesus
From his body it departed,
Yet, when he was raised up to
heaven,
In body and soul it ascended.

12

Al pie de la cruz sentada,
con el cuerpo de Jesús,
lo tiene en sus santos brazos
aquella hermosa luz.

12

At the foot of the cross she is seated,
With the body of her son,
She holds him in her holy arms,
The most brilliant light of all.

13

13

El corazón dividido,
de verlo que padeció
y su santísima madre,
los huérfanos convidó.

Divided is her heart,
Her son in corporal affliction,
And his most holy mother
Gave the orphans an invitation.

14

Llorar, cristianos, llorar,
llorar ésta triste suerte,
llorar hasta la muerte
con María en su soledad.

14

Cry, Christians, cry,
Cry for this sad fate,
Cry until death's date,
With Mary in her solitude.

15

Todo se me va en llorar,
sólo en pensar en Jesús,
que por redimir
al hombre,
quiso morir en la cruz.

15

All my time is spent in sorrow,
Thinking of my Lord unceasingly,
That to redeem all people for
tomorrow,
On the cross he died so willingly.

16

Las puertas del cielo abiertas
ya Jesús resucitó,
visitó el seno del limbo,
los santos padres sacó.

16

The heavenly gates are opened,
Jesus has arisen,
He visited the depths of Limbo,
The holy fathers he has released.

17

17

✝ 11 ✝

Estaba Junto al Madero
She Was Standing Near the Timber

Estaba junto al madero and *Estabas Madre Dolorosa* (You Were Standing, Sorrowful Mother) are two distinct New Mexican versions of the *Stabat Mater*, a Latin hymn probably of thirteenth-century origin. The *Stabat Mater* has been attributed to St. Bonaventure and Pope Innocent II, but most scholars credit Jacopone Da Todi with the work. Others dispute this attribution, claiming the poem is much older.

The *Stabat Mater* has a regular meter, most often trochaic, and an intricate rhyme scheme some scholars date to the twelfth century: a-a-b-c-c-b.[66]

Stabat Mater dolorosa,	The mother all filled with sorrow,
Juxta crucem lacrymosa,	Near the cross could be found crying
Dum pendebat Filius.	Where her son hung up above.
Cujus animam gementem,	She whose spirit groaned with sighing,
Contristatam et dolentem,	So contrite and filled with pain,
Pertransivit gladius.	Pierced by the sword of a mother's love.

A Spanish version, possibly a medieval translation, is entitled *La Madre estaba llorosa* (The Mother Was Standing Weeping). This version, along with the original Latin version, was carried by the Franciscans to the New World and clearly influenced the New Mexican alabados.

La Madre estaba llorosa	The Mother was standing weeping
junto a la cruz dolorosa,	Near the cross she was grieving,
de donde su hijo colgaba:	Where her son hung up above:
A cuya alma es tanta pena	Whose soul in so much sorrow
de tristeza y dolor llena,	Filled with such sadness and pain,
dura espada atravesaba.	Ran the sword of suffering love.

The New Mexican version reads,

Estabas, Madre	You were standing, sorrowful
dolorosa,	mother,
al pie de la cruz llorosa	At the foot of the cross weeping
donde pende el Redentor.	Where the Redeemer hung above.
1	1
Cuyo espíritu paciente	In your spirit, though so patient,
traspasada vivamente	Pierced with anguish unrelenting,
una espada de dolor.	Ran the sword of suffering love.
2	2

Many of the Penitente alabados in the tradition of the *Stabat Mater* exalt the Mother of Christ and trace in narrative form the foundation of Christianity through the sufferings and the death of Jesus Christ. *Estaba junto al madero*, which consists of quatrains with the rhyme scheme a-b-b-a, is a beautiful rendition of this basic theme. It begins by describing Our Lady's pain as she saw her son suffer and die on the cross: "Her broken heart was pierced with pain upon seeing him crucified, as had been prophesied in ancient times." The penitent begs of Our Lady to "let me feel the pain in your heart and the pain of your son's wounds because I too share in the guilt of his death." The penitent then offers his penance and pain for the atonement of his sins. In the last stanza he asks for the Blessed Mother's help, if he should die, in ensuring that his soul will reach the Heavenly Kingdom.

Estaba junto al madero, *de la cruz la dolorosa,* *madre de Jesús llorosa,* *viendo pendiente al Cordero.*	She was standing near the timber Of the cross where she was grieving, The mother of Christ was weeping, Seeing the Lamb of God hanging.
1	1
Cuya alma triste gemía *traspasada por el rigor* *de la espada del dolor* *de la antigua profecía.*	Her soul was sadly wailing, Impaled with such severity By the sword of sorrowfulness, By the ancient prophesying.
2	2
¡Cuán triste y con qué aflicción, *aquella madre bendita* *del unigénito imita,* *compasiva la cruel pasión!*	How sad and afflicted with pain Was the Blessed Mother, Like her only begotten, Like him in his cruel passion!
3	3
Tiembla ya la mujer fuerte *al ver al ínclito Hijo* *luchar en el leño fijo* *con la más terrible muerte.*	The vigorous woman quakes, On seeing her son hanging, On the fixed lumber struggling, In terrible death throes.
4	4
¡Quién en el llanto no *rompiera* *si la inocente madre* *de Cristo ofrecerlo* *al Padre* *en tanto suplicio viera!*	Who would not join her in her lament If the most innocent Mother Of Christ, offering him to the Heavenly Father, In such torment was observed!
5	5

¡Quién no se contristara
si a la madre piadosa
con su Hijo dolorosa,
juntamente contemplara!

Who would not be moved
If the mother in consolation,
With her son in desolation,
Together they were viewed!

6

Por pecados de su gente,
vío a Jesús en tormentos
y sujeto a azotes cruentos,
como esclavo delincuente,

For the sin of all mankind,
She saw Jesus in torment
And whipped till he was bleeding,
Like a delinquent slave.

7

Moribundo y desolado,
vió a su dulce Hijo María
cuando al Padre Eterno envía
su espíritu encomendado.

While dying desolated,
Mary saw her sweet son
When to the Heavenly Father he sent
And entrusted his spirit.

8

¡Ea, Madre, fuente de amor,
para que con vos lloremos,
haced que participemos
la fuerza de este dolor!

Listen, Mother, fountain of affection,
So that we can be in tears
And participate as peers
In the strength of this pain!

9

Haz mi corazón arder
de amor en viva hoguera
de Cristo, Dios, de manera
que le pueda complacer.

Make my heart burn
With the living fire of love
Of Christ, God, in a manner
That is pleasing to him.

10

Esto, santa Madre, hagas
y del que ves en el leño;
fija también con empeño
en mi corazón las llagas.

This, Holy Mother, do to me
As to the one you see on the cross;
Fix with eagerness as you should
All the wounds in the heart.

11

Pues son tantas y no ajenas
de mí por quien se ha dignado
ser herido y maltratado,
parte conmigo sus penas.

12

Haz que mi alma, condolida,
llore, verdaderamente
contigo, o Cristo pendiente
de la cruz, toda mi vida.

13

Contigo de noche y día,
junto del madero santo,
acompañando tu llanto,
de buena gana estaría.

14

Virgen, sobre todas pura,
lloro tu dolor contigo,
no seas amarga conmigo,
pues eres toda dulzura.

15

Haz que, por imitación
de Cristo llagas y muerte,
transporte en mí con la suerte
de su afrentosa pasión.

16

En la misma cruz llagado,
con sus heridas me vio,
por amor de tu Hijo yo sea
de su néctar embriagado.

17

My faults are mine and no one else's,
Faults which he has condescended
To be injured and maltreated,
Divide with me your pains.

12

Make my pain-filled soul
Cry truly
With you, oh Christ hanging
From the cross, all of my life.

13

With you night and day,
Near the holy timber,
Accompanying you in your sorrow,
This would be my desire.

14

Virgin, above all so pure,
I cry in pain with you,
Please don't be bitter with me,
You are filled with sweetness.

15

Deign that by imitation
Of Christ's wounds and death
I will be transported by fate
In your humiliating passion.

16

On the same cross hanging wounded,
With his injuries he saw me,
For your son's love I will be
By his nectar intoxicated.

17

Inflamado y enardecido
de amor, por este suplicio
de Jesús, sea el día del juicio
por ti, Virgen, defendido.

18

Sellado con eficacia
de la cruz sea la muerte,
la de Cristo, mi escudo fuerte,
que me asegura la gracia.

19

Haz en tu reino memoria
de mí cuando el cuerpo muera,
porque a mi alma se confiara
al paraíso de la Gloria.

20

Inflamed and impassioned
With love, for this torment
Of Jesus', on the day of judgment
By you, Virgin, I will be defended.

18

Sealed with efficiency
Of the cross is the passing
Of Christ, his shield embracing,
That assures me of his grace.

19

In your kingdom have a memory
Of me when my body dies,
So that my soul resides
In the Paradise of Glory.

20

✞ 12 ✞

A Mi Señor de Esquípulas
To My Lord of Esquípulas

The veneration of Christ as the Lord of Esquípulas occurs in only two regions of the world, New Mexico and southeastern Guatemala. In the Guatemalan town of Esquípulas there is a large wooden crucifix known as *Nuestro Señor de Esquípulas* (Our Lord of Esquípulas). This crucifix is recognized throughout the country as a miraculous image. Quirio Catano, a Portuguese sculptor, was commissioned to make it in 1595. Catano carved the crucifix out of balsam and orange wood, painted the cross green, and embellished it with gold leaf.

The Indians readily accepted the crucifix, since the skin coloring of the Christ figure closely resembled their own (after years of being in a room with burning candles, the figure turned smoky black in hue). Miraculous cures were attributed to the crucifix as well as to the earth nearby, which was collected by the faithful and either eaten or mixed with water and drunk. In New Mexico, the same custom was followed at the Santuario de Chimayó. Here, also, is a miraculous crucifix entitled *Nuestro Señor de Esquípulas*, and the nearby earth is thought to have healing powers. The veneration of Christ as Señor de Esquípulas was apparently introduced into New Mexico by Bernardo Abeyta, an influential Penitente leader and Hermano Mayor in 1814, and it apparently served as the inspiration for this alabado.

In the alabado, the penitent asks the Lord of Esquípulas to help him persevere in his penance. He feels that even if the will to do penance is present, the devil is always near, tempting all Christians away from their duties. The penitent asks that, through the divine intercession of the Blessed Virgin, the Señor de Esquípulas bless and have mercy on him. After a few stanzas in which the penitent recites parts of the Passion, he states that he must cope with the memory of the suffering of the Lord of Esquípulas but believes Christ is always merciful. In the last stanza, the penitent offers his prayerful hymn for the souls blessed by God and for those who have sinned against him.

A mi Señor de Esquípulas,
en vuestras duras tinieblas,
danos la mano ahora,
en el cielo y en la tierra,

1

To my Lord of Esquípulas,
In our terrible darkness,
Give us your hand today,
In heaven and on earth.

1

El demonio perturbando,
el pecado del cristiano,
pues mi Señor de Esquípulas,
lo retira con su mano.

2

The demon causing
The sin of the Christian,
Well, my Lord of Esquípulas
With his hand, heals the lesion.

2

Por la corona de espinas,
con que fuiste coronado,
mi corazón es obligado,
y el de mi Dios consagrado.

3

For the crown of thorns
With which you were coronated,
My heart to my God
Is obliged and consecrated.

3

Todo viviente cristiano,
que cree en la virgen pura,
alabamos y ensalzamos,
a mi Señor de Esquípulas.

4

All living Christians
Who believe in the purity of Mary
Praise and extol
My Lord of Esquípulas.

4

<table>
<tr><td>Pues con sus benditas manos,
nos eche su bendición,
la emperatriz de los cielos,
y la santa comunión.</td><td>Well, with her blessed hands,
May she bless us all indeed,
The Empress of the Heavens,
Give us communion in our need.</td></tr>
<tr><td>5</td><td>5</td></tr>
<tr><td>Pues la reina de los cielos,
camina una noche obscura,
ten de nosotros piedad,
Padre Señor de Esquípulas.</td><td>Well, the Queen of the Heavens,
On a dark night travel,
On all of us show your pity,
Father, Lord of Esquípulas.</td></tr>
<tr><td>6</td><td>6</td></tr>
<tr><td>Por las caídas que va dando,
en la calle de amargura,
vamos todos alabando,
a mi Señor de Esquípulas.</td><td>For the falls that he takes,
On the street of bitterness,
Let us all sing hymns,
To my Lord of Esquípulas.</td></tr>
<tr><td>7</td><td>7</td></tr>
<tr><td>Por el dolor que sintió,
cuando en la cruz lo clavaron,
boca abajo lo pusieron,
y los clavos remacharon.</td><td>For the pain that he felt,
When they nailed him to the cross,
Face down they turned him
And the nails hammered down.</td></tr>
<tr><td>8</td><td>8</td></tr>
<tr><td>Pues por la sangre de Cristo,
que se imprime en mi memoria,
Padre Señor de Esquípulas.
convídanos con tu gloria.</td><td>Well, for the blood of Christ,
That's imprinted on my memory,
Father, Lord of Esquípulas,
Surround us with your glory.</td></tr>
<tr><td>9</td><td>9</td></tr>
<tr><td>Todos los que tengan fe,
esperanza y caridad,
pues mi Señor de Esquípulas.
ten de nosotros piedad.</td><td>All of you who have faith,
Hope, and benevolence,
Well, my Lord of Esquípulas,
Have mercy on all of us.</td></tr>
<tr><td>10</td><td>10</td></tr>
</table>

Lidiando con su memoria
daremos gracias a Dios
yesperamos que en la gloria
juntos nos vayamos con vos.

11

A mi Señor de Esquípulas,
yo le ofresco este alabado
por las ánimas benditas
y las que están en pecado.

12

In dealing with his memory,
We'll give thanks to our Lord,
And hope that in Paradise,
Together we will go in accord.

11

To my Lord of Esquípulas,
I offer up this hymn,
For the blessed souls,
And for those in sin.

12

✝ 13 ✝

PADRE JESÚS NAZARENO
FATHER JESUS OF NAZARETH

In rapid succession, the writer of this beautifully harmonious ballad relates the scenes of the Passion. In the final stanza he states that it is everyone's duty to sing about the sufferings of Christ on every Friday.

Padre Jesús Nazareno,	Father Jesus of Nazareth,
que queréis haga de mí,	Do as you will with me,
alabando a tu poder	Praising your supreme power
y suspirando por ti.	And yearning for you.
1	1
Ya le amarranron los brazos	They already restrained your arms
y lo clavaron en la cruz	And nailed you to the cross,
le remacharon los clavos	They clinched those nails
a nuestro Padre Jesús.	To secure you, Father Lord Jesus.
2	2
Ya le echan la soga al cuello	They tied you from the neck
y lo llevan arrastrando;	And pulled you dragging;
a nuestro Padre Jesús	Our Father Lord Jesus
ya lo van martirizando.	They have martyred.
3	3
Le ponen en la cabeza	They place on his head
una corona de espinas,	A crown of thorns,
y se le entierran las puntas	And the spines dig into
en esas sienes divinas.	His most divine temples.
4	4

Madre mia de los dolores
ya lo llevan a tu Hijo amado,
sudando gotas de sangre
sobre ese manto dorado.

5

My mother of sorrows
They have taken your beloved son,
Sweating drops of blood,
Over that golden mantel.

5

Simón Cirineo ayuda
a soliviarle la cruz,
y yo me quedo mirando
a nuestro padre Jesús.

6

Simon the Cyreniac helps
To raise the cross,
And I can only watch,
My Father Lord Jesus.

6

Válgame Dios de los cielos,
ya lo llevan los judíos;
le dan con la disciplina,
¿qué haremos, hermanos míos?

7

Good God of the heavens,
They take you
And lash you with the whip.
What can we do, brothers of mine?

7

Madre mía de los dolores,
ya llevas un desconsuelo,
que van para la parroquia
con tu Hijo cayendo al suelo.

8

My mother of sorrows,
In so much affliction,
They go to the congregation
With your son falling to the ground.

8

Mira que lo están velando
como al sol acrisolado,
todos aquellos armados
lo hicieron ser coronado.

9

See how we hold his wake,
Like the sun purifying,
Those who were armed
Forced him to be crowned.

9

Madre mía de los dolores,
eres punto de la guía
¿dónde encontraste a tu Hijo
el viernes santo a medio día?

10

My mother of sorrows,
You are the guide,
Where did you find your son
At noon on Holy Friday?

10

Aquí acabo de decir
toda la pasión de Cristo
porque los viernes se alaba
la sangre de Jesucristo.

11

Here I stop recounting
The passion of Christ
Because every Friday is praised
The blood of Jesus Christ.

11

✞ 14 ✞

Cristo Caminaba
Christ Traveled

This touching ballad describes the final moments of the Passion. The redemption of our sins through the death of Christ is emphasized in stanzas 12 and 13.

Cristo caminaba	Christ traveled
haciendo oración	Deep in prayer
cuando Jesucristo	When the Redeemer
sintio su aflicción.	Felt his affliction.
1	1
Al Monte Calvario	Toward Mount Calvary,
con la cruz pesada	With a heavy cross,
su madre lo encuentra	His mother encounters him
muy maravillada.	Full of wonder.
2	2
Su madre se aflije	His mother is anguished
de ver a Jesús	On seeing her son,
que no hay quien le quite	There is no one who can take away
la pesada cruz.	the heavy cross.
3	3
Jesús se enternece	Jesus is moved
de ver a su madre,	On seeing his mother,
no hay quien la consuele,	No one to console her,
de verlo en su sangre.	On seeing his blood.
4	4

Que sangre virtuosa,
sale dando luz,
que los pecadores
mueran por Jesús.

What virtuous blood,
Flows giving light,
So that all sinners
May die for Christ.

5

Jesús aflijido
con grande ternura,
la muerte de Cristo
en la sepultura.

Jesus is afflicted,
But with great kindness
He meets his death
And is laid to rest.

6

El sol se obscurece
con grande dolor,
la luna se enluta
por nuestro Señor.

The sun darkens
With so much ardor,
The moon mourns
For our dear Savior.

7

Estrellas alisadas,
que ya no dan luz,
que todas sintieron
a nuestro Señor.

Mangled stars
No longer glimmer,
They all feel pain
For our Redeemer.

8

La sábana santa
le echan al costado
en donde Jesús
a resucitado.

The holy shroud
Is laid at the side
Where our Lord Jesus
Has been resurrected.

9

El Señor está
clavado en la cruz
todos nos postramos
al ver a Jesús.

Our Lord is Nailed
On the cross,
We all kneel down
On seeing Jesus.

10

Bendito el Señor,
que nos dio su luz,
todos lo aclamamos,
al pie de la cruz.

Blessed is our Lord
Who gave us his light,
We all cry for him
At the foot of the cross.

11

Adiós mi Jesús,
cargado de llagas,
que al pie de la cruz,
fueron remediadas.

Goodbye, my Jesus,
Full of affliction,
At the foot of the cross,
We find redemption.

12

Adiós mi Jesús
que eres primoroso,
llevanos al cielo,
con eterno gozo.

Goodbye, my Jesus,
Every so holy,
Please take us to heaven,
To bathe in your glory.

13

Nuestro Señor de Esquípulas *(Our Lord of Esquípulas). Crucifix by Horacio Valdéz. Twentieth-century, New Mexico. De Aragón family collection.*

✝ 15 ✝
Mi Dios y Mi Redentor
My God and My Redeemer

Upon first reading this beautiful alabado, we are astonished at the simplicity of expression, the elevation of sentiments, and the formal perfection of the work. The poem, which is very carefully structured, begins with an introduction to the contents and concludes with a direct appeal to the sentiments and conscience of the listeners. The rhyme scheme is a-b-b-a-a-c. The sixth line in each stanza is unrhymed with other lines in the stanza, but all of the last lines rhyme with each other: *amor, Señor, sudor,* etc.

The theme is delineated in the beginning of the second stanza:

Escucha con atención	Listen with attention
lo que padeció Jesús	To what Jesus suffered for us
desde el huerto hasta la cruz.	From the garden to the cross.

Stanzas 3 to 27 provide a detailed description of the scenes of the Passion—a description often characterized by genuine originality. Note this example from stanza 23:

Los pies se los barrenaron	Then his feet were drilled
para clavarlo mejor.	To make nailing easier.

And stanza 24 presents us with this curious detail:

Después que asi lo enclavaron,	After he had been thus nailed,
como tan mal lo quisieron,	Since he was so disliked,
boca abajo lo volvieron	Face down he was flipped,
y los clavos remacharon.	And the nails were flattened.

A descriptive liveliness is apparent throughout the alabado, along with a sweet simplicity, an exactness of expression, and a human sentimentality. The obvious intention is to motivate the repentance of personal sins by portraying the suffering of the Savior at every stage of the Passion.

Mi Dios y mi Redentor,	My God and my Redeemer,
en quien espero y confío	In whom I trust and have faith,
por tu pasión,	Through your passion, my dear
Dios mió,	Lord,
abrázame en vuestro amor.	Embrace me in your love.
1	1
Escucha con atención	Listen with attention
lo que padeció Jesús,	To what Jesus suffered for us
desde el huerto hasta la cruz.	From the garden to the cross.
En su sagrada pasión;	For the Lord's most sacred Passion,
lágrimas de devoción	May we shed tears of devotion
nos dé a todos el Señor.	For what he gave for us.
2	2
Afligido y angustiado,	Afflicted and tormented,
lo verás en la oración	You shall see him in this oration
y sintiendo su pasión.	And feel mournful for his Passion.
Sangre en el huerto ha sudado,	In the garden, blood he sweated,
hasta la tierra ha llegado	Onto the earth it descended,
lo copioso del sudor.	So profuse was his anguish.
3	3
En la prisión lo arrastraron	Through the prison he was herded,
y a los brazos con cordeles	With bound arms pulled so brutally,
echándole lazos crueles	Whipped with lashes cruelly,
la sangre le reventaron.	His blood spurted,
Y así preso lo llevaron	And, as a prisoner, he was treated
como a un hombre malhechor.	As a man who has done wrong.
4	4

A la mejilla inocente,
con mano de hierro armada,
dan tan recio bofetada
que hacen que en sangre
reviente.
Mi Dios, pues el alma siente
ser causa de tal rigor.

On the innocent cheek,
With a hand armed swiftly,
A blow is given quickly,
And the blood is soon
set free,
But the guilt is deep within me
For such cruelty, my Lord.

5

¡Oh, quién estuviese allí,
dulce amante y dueño mío,
y al golpe de aquel judío
pusiera el rostro por ti!
Toda la culpa está
en mí
y vos lo pagáis, Señor.

Oh, if only I could have been with
My sweet and loving Master,
You were struck by that one Jew,
I'd have put my face in place of
yours!
All the guilt is within me
And you have paid for it, my Lord.

6

Con furia y rabia es
llevado
de uno en otro tribunal
y lo miraron tan . . .
que de loco lo han tratado
y con Barrabás mirado,
dicen que Jesús es peor.

With fury and rage you've been
treated,
From one tribunal to another,
They have seen you, as a bother,
As a crazy man mistreated,
And with Barabbas
Proclaiming you the worse.

7

Desnudo está y azotado
con tan terrible fiereza
que desde el pie a la cabeza
lo verás todo llagado.
¡Oh, qué caro la ha costado
el querer al pecador!

He is stripped and scourged
With such terrible fierceness
That from his feet up to his head
You shall see him wounded.
Oh, how dearly he has suffered
For his love of the sinner!

8

Con penetrantes espinas
coronaron su cabeza
y, apretándolas con fuerza,
rompen las sienes divinas,
abriéndose así las minas
del oro de más valor.

9

En el balcón asomado,
"¡Ecce homo!" dice Pilatos,
y responde el pueblo ingrato,
"¡Que muera crucificado!"
Que aun con verlo tan
llagado
no está saciado el rencor.

10

Insta el pueblo porfiado
sobre que Jesús muriera.
¡Oh, mi Dios, quién tal creyera
que Tú fueses sentenciado
a morir crucificado,
siendo de la vida autor!

11

Con un pesado
madero,
descalzo y todo llagado,
va de espinas coronado
el manifiesto cordero.
También tira un
sayón fiero
de la soga con furor.

12

With penetrating spines
His head was crowned,
And pressing them with force
They tore the temples so divine,
Thus cutting open mines
Of the most precious gold.

9

On the balcony held in view,
"Ecce Homo!" Pilate uttered,
And the demanding audience shouted,
"Let him die crucified!"
Even upon seeing him completely
wounded
Their animosity still lingered.

10

The stubborn crowd specified
That it is Jesus who must die.
Oh, my Lord, who will believe
That you should be sentenced
To die crucified,
Being that you are the giver of life!

11

Carrying the instrument for
execution,
Wounded and barefooted,
He goes painfully coronated,
As the manifest lamb.
The ugly executioner pulls without
explanation
The rope with injurious fury.

12

El cuerpo lleva inclinado
y las mejillas hermosas
con salivas asquerosas
y el rostro acardenalado,
denegrido y afeador,
va que el verlo es un dolor.

13

Se oye el falso pregonero
que al eco de la trompeta,
estando todos alerta,
dice que es un embustero
y que muera el hechicero
en una cruz por traidor.

14

Ya lo han traído a empellones
con rigor fiero o inhumano,
y en ves de darle la mano,
le dieron de puntillones
y con golpes evicciones
levantan a su Señor.

15

Al encuentro le ha salido
la madre que le parió
y entre sayones
le vío,
arrastrado y escupido;
su corazón fué partido
con espada de dolor.

16

He carries his body inclined,
And the face once so handsome
Is covered with loathsome saliva
And his countenance is blackened,
Afflicted, and misshapened,
Oh my, to see him is so painful.

13

The harbinger is calling
With the echo of the trumpet
So that everyone is alerted.
He accuses the bewitcher of lying,
And he is sentenced to die
On a cross as a traitor.

14

They brought him in and assaulted
Him with inhuman raging fury,
And instead of being given a hand,
With their feet he was tormented,
And with heavy blows was evicted,
And that is how they picked him up.

15

In a sudden meeting there appeared
The mother who bore you,
And between executioners
she did see
You dragged and jeered at,
And her heart was pierced
By a sword of pain.

16

Un cirineo han hallado
que ayude a llevar la cruz,
porque temen que Jesús
muera y no crucificado,
por esto se lo han
buscado,
no por piedad ni favor.

17

Lleno de polvo y sudado
la Verónica le ha visto,
y, limpiando el rostro a Cristo,
en el lienzo fué estampado.
Bien se le pagó el cuidado
porque es muy buen pagador.

18

Llega con la cruz pesada
al Calvario y con presteza
le quitaron con fiereza
la vestidura sagrada,
la carne salió pegada
a la túnica interior.

19

Desnudo y arrodillado
y a la vista de su madre,
se ofrece por ti a
Dios Padre,
en caridad abrasado.
Hiel y vinagre le han
dado
para tormento mayor.

20

They found a Cyreniac
To help with the cross,
For they feared your death
Before your crucifixion,
And that was the reason for their
attention,
Not charity or kindness.

17

In dust and sweat enveloped,
To Veronica he appeared,
And when his face was cleansed,
On the cloth it became imprinted.
For her care she was rewarded,
As he is a generous redeemer.

18

When he, a heavy cross bearing,
Arrived at Calvary, they quickly
And fiercely pulled away
His most sacred clothing,
With flesh still clinging
To the inside of his vestments.

19

On his knees and without clothing
And in sight of his mother,
He offered himself for you to God
the Father,
With his love still burning.
With gall and vinegar they were
yearning
To torment him on the cross.

20

En la cruz ya recostado,
verás de un clavo tirano,
la punta en su diestra mano
y un martillo levantado.
¡Oh, qué golpe ha descargado
que hace temblar al creador!

21

A la siniestra le echaron
lazos con unos cordeles
y tirando muy crueles
los huesos desencajaron.
Nuevos golpes resonaron
al clavarlo con furor.

22

También las piernas ataron
y estando el cuerpo encogido,
tiran tanto que extendido
todo lo descoyuntaron.
Los pies se los barrenaron
para clavarlo mejor.

23

Después que así lo enclavaron,
como tan mal lo quiesieron,
boca abajo lo volvieron
y los clavos remacharon.
Las llagas las arrastraron
sin piedad y sin temor.

24

On the cross he was placed,
And a cruel nail in the joint
Of the right hand was planted
And the hammer poised.
Oh, what a blow was delivered,
And it made the Creator tremble!

21

Around his left hand they girded
Cords to tie it back,
And pulling they did wrack
The bones which were disjointed.
New blows were repeated
As they hammered furiously.

22

His legs were also tied
And his body being contracted,
They pulled so hard that
Everything was dislocated.
Then his feet were drilled
To make nailing easier.

23

After he had been thus nailed,
Since he was so disliked,
Face down he was flipped
And the nails were flattened.
The wounds were lacerated
Without pity or respect.

24

En alto está levantado,
blasfemado de sayones,
y en medio de los ladrones,
sediento y desamparado.
Su cuerpo está destrozado
y denegrido el color.

25

Way up high he was raised,
Blasphemed by the bailiffs,
And in between two thieves,
Thirsty and half dazed.
His body traumatized
And bruised.

25

El sol ya se ha obscurecido,
la tierra ya se ve temblando,
el velo se va rasgando
y las piedras hacen ruido.
El mundo está conmovido
cuando muere el Salvador.

26

The sun has darkened,
The earth is trembling,
As the veil is tearing
And the rocks are shaken.
The whole world is awakened
When the Savior dies.

26

Un atrevido soldado,
viendo que Jesús ha muerto,
con una lanza le ha abierto
el santísimo costado.
Agua y sangre ha derramado
para bien del pecador.

27

An insolent soldier boldly,
Seeing that Jesus has died,
With his spear has pried
Open the side most holy,
Spilling water and blood which solely
Was shed for the good of the sinner.

27

Haced, Señor soberano,
que en esa llaga de amor
se abrase en divino ardor
todo corazón cristiano
y todo el género humano
os confiese Redentor.

28

Sovereign Lord, please allow
That in that wound of love
A flame of divine ardor from above
Will fill each Christian heart
And all mankind will take part.
Grant this be so, my Redeemer.

28

Y haced, mi Jesús amado,
que mis ojos, hechos fuente,
lloren lágrimas ardientes
de lo mucho que he pecado,
y pues tanto os ha costado
y sois liberal dador.

29

My loving Jesus, always so enduring,
Make my eyes into fountains flowing
With fervent tears burning
Because of my sinning
And for your suffering,
For you are a generous Redeemer.

29

Nuestro Padre Jesús Nazareno *(Our Father Jesus of Nazareth), by José Benito Ortega. Nineteenth-century, Mora, New Mexico. De Aragón family collection.*

✝ 16 ✝

Cristo Nuestro Redentor
Christ Is Our Redeemer

This alabado is basically a prayer, but it contains several stanzas that narrate incidents of the Passion. It consists of quatrains in which the second and fourth lines usually rhyme and the first and third sometimes do.

Cristo, nuestro Redentor;	Christ is our Redeemer,
Cristo, nuestra companía;	Christ is our coadjutor,
Cristo, nuestro Salvador;	Christ is our dear Savior,
Cristo, nuestro amparo y guía.	Christ is our guide and mentor.
1	1
Fue escupido entre sayones,	His executioners spat upon him
con salivas asquerosas,	With saliva, oh so loathsome,
con grillos y con cadenas	Bound him with shackles and chains
y remachadas esposas.	And with clinching manacles.
2	2
Ya vienen los fariseos,	The Pharisees arriving
a cometer el pecado	To commit their sole disgrace,
en busca de mi Jesús	Our dear Jesus they all search for,
un Señor sacramentado.	Our most holy sacrifice.
3	3
A este Padre verdadero	To this true father they
le dan una bofetada,	Give blows across his face,
viendo que no se había muerto,	And seeing that he is not dying,
le dieron una lanzada.	They pierce him with a sword.
4	4

Su madre con santo celo
traspasada de dolor
contempla en sus santas llagas
y su divina pasión.

5

Estos clavos penetrantes
y esta corona de espinas
fueron las que traspasaron
hasta sus sienes divinas.

6

Le dieron hiel y vinagre
todos con mala intención,
le rompieron las entrañas
a mi Dios y Redentor.

7

Este niño que pariste,
madre, con tanto
dolor,
este es el que está
pagando
la culpa del pecador.

8

No estés triste, madre mía,
no te metas en cuidados,
aunque veas a tu Hijo
que está muerto y sepultado.

9

His mother with such devotion,
Heavily laden with her pain,
Contemplates his holy affliction
And his passion most divine.

5

These penetrating nails
And this crown of spiny thorns
Were thus so firmly planted
That his flesh was ripped and torn.

6

Gall and vinegar they gave him,
With bad intentions in mind,
They broke his innermost being,
My Redeemer most divine.

7

This son that you gave birth to,
Sorrowful Mother, with so
much pain,
He is the one who must pay
the debt
For the sinner, yours and mine.

8

Don't be sad, my dear Mother,
Don't allow yourself apprehension,
Even though you may see our Savior
Dead after so much affliction.

9

Al tercer día salió
de aquel sepulcro sagrado,
y el pecador queda libre,
de la culpa y el pecado.

On the third day he departed
From that most sacred burial place,
The sinner was liberated
From all blame and sacrilege.

10

Nuestra madre intercesora
que alaba la luz del día,
canten los dulces nombres
dolores de María.

10

Our dear Mother intercessor
Who praises the light of day,
Sing the praises of those sweet
Pains of the Blessed Mother Mary.

11

Padre di misericordia,
Padre de mi corazón,
que conoció al mundo entero
con su sagrada pasión.

11

Father of mercy,
Father of my heart,
Who knows all the earth
With his most sacred passion.

12

A la reina soberana,
Madre de mi Redentor,
sea nuestro amparo y guía,
también nuestra intercesión.

12

To the Sovereign Queen,
Mother of my redemption,
Be our protector and guide
And aid us by your intercession.

13

Este pesado madero
que ha traído nuestro Señor
es por el pecado feo
que cometió el pecador.

13

You know this heavy cross
That our dear Savior carried,
It is for our most dreadful sin
That he made his commitment to us.

14

Ese niño prodigioso
y mi Dios sacramentado
es el que se ha hecho redentor
de la culpa y del
pecado.

14

That exquisite little infant
And my God, the Blessed Sacrament,
It is he who has redeemed
Our sin and become our
chastisement.

15

15

Su madre como piadosa
con su buena intercesión,
se duela de nuestras almas
por su infinita pasión.

16

Esta madre enternecida,
te aclama con alegría
y cree que ha de venir
a estar en su companía.

17

Madre reina soberana,
perdóname por tu amor,
sea nuestro amparo y guía,
también nuestra redención.

18

Su madre compadecida,
traspasada de dolor,
le pide a su amado
Hijo
que perdone al pecador.

19

Aclamemos tu
poder,
Padre de misericordia,
líbranos del ángel malo
y llévanos a tu gloria.

20

His mother who is most merciful,
With her most holy intercession,
Takes charge of our souls
Because of her infinite compassion.

16

This most affectionate mother,
Cries out to us with such happiness
And feels she must be our intercessor
And accompany us in our loneliness.

17

Oh, most Sovereign Queen,
With all your love you must forgive
And be my sanction and protection
So that I too may live.

18

His mother, in her holiness,
Is touched with grief and compassion
And pleads with her son, in loving
kindness,
To forgive the sinner in his passion.

19

With your power, which we
acclaim,
Oh, most merciful Father,
Free us from condemnation
And take us to you in heaven.

20

Esta madre verdadera,
madre llena de dolor,
le mira sus santas
llagas
a mi Dios y Redentor.

21

Esta madre estimativa,
Madre llena de dolor,
contempla su santa
muerte
que tuvo nuestro Señor.

22

Madres, las que tengan hijos,
contemplen este dolor,
hagan llanto por su amado,
ya murió nuestro Señor.

23

Vi a mi Dios coronado,
clavado en la santa cruz;
Oigamos con dulce llanto,
"Padre nuestro, amén, Jesús."

24

Este Cristo y este santo
relicario del Señor,
con el espíritu santo,
échanos tu bendición.

25

The Blessed Mother
I know is so forlorn,
She contemplates the wounds of
Jesus
And her dear heart is torn.

21

This most honorable mother,
I know is so forlorn,
She contemplates the death of
Jesus
Who by her was borne.

22

Mothers, who have children,
Contemplate this pain in love,
And cry for this most loved one,
For he has died, our precious dove.

23

I saw my Savior crowned,
Nailed on the sacred cross;
Hear our doleful singing,
"God our Father, amen, Jesus."

24

This Christ and holy relic
Of our Savior in his passion,
And with the Holy Spirit,
Give us your benediction.

25

La Purisima Concepción *(Immaculate Conception), by J. Guadalupe Góngora. Nineteenth-century engraving, Mexico. De Aragón family collection.*

✞ 17 ✞

Bendito el Santo Madero
Blessed Is the Holy Beam

The veneration of the cross is the theme of this heart-rending alabado. It serves to remind all Christians of the symbol that signifies the death of Jesus but also his Resurrection. The cross was an ancient instrument of execution, and because of the Crucifixion of Jesus it became the emblem of Christianity.

The earliest known image of Christ's figure on the cross, a miniature contained in a Syrian codex of the Gospels written by the scribe Rabula, dates back to A.D. 586. The true cross itself was allegedly discovered in A.D. 362 by St. Helena, the mother of Constantine, and minute pieces were distributed throughout the Christian world for purposes of adoration.

In *Bendito el santo madero*, all Christians are asked to adore the cross and concentrate on its redeeming powers. The fourth stanza states, "No tree has ever been as strong as that used to make the holy beam, for on it hung all of mankind's sin and on it Christ met his death." Stanza 6 reads, "Christ died for us so that we may live in his light, and he left us the holy cross as our defense."

Bendito el santo madero,	Blessed is the holy beam,
árbol de la santa cruz,	Tree of the crucifixion,
donde fuimos redimidos	Where our sins were all redeemed
con sangre de mi Jesús.	With the blood of my dear Jesus.
1	1

En la cruz mi Redentor
con tres clavos fue clavado,
allí quedó enarbolado
el cuerpo de mi Jesús.

2

Oíd cristianos pecadores
la muerte de mi Jesús,
que por tenernos amor
quiso morir en la cruz.

3

No se verá árbol tan fuerte
como el del santo madero,
pues ocupó al mundo entero,
Cristo en él tuvo su muerte.

4

Si el enemigo y la culpa
lo tuvieron prisionero,
Cristo en el santo madero,
la muerte eterna indultó.

5

Cristo murió por nosotros
para que vivamos en luz,
y nos dejó en nuestra defensa
a la Santísima Cruz.

6

Hállese al confesor,
cristiano busca la luz,
y el madero de la cruz,
él será tu defensor.

7

On the cross my sweet Redeemer
With three nails was sustained,
On there was suspended
The body of my Jesus.

2

Hear, Christians unrepentant,
Of the death of my dear Jesus,
Because he loved us all so dearly,
Willingly dying, his life ceases.

3

No tree has been as strong
As that used to make the holy
beam,
For on it hung all of mankind's sin
And on it Christ met his death.

4

If the enemy and sin
Kept him prisoner,
Christ on the holy beam
Conquered eternal death.

5

Christ died for us
So we may live in light,
And he left in our defense
The most holy cross.

6

Find the confessor,
Christians search for the light,
And the beam of the cross
Shall be your own defender.

7

En fin Santísima Cruz
yo me despido de ti,
cuando Dios me llame a juicio,
ruega a mi Cristo por mí.

8

In the end, holy cross,
I depart from you,
When God calls me to judgment,
Pray to Christ for me.

8

La cruz está en la custodia
y la hostia en la cruz está,
y en el juicio universal,
la Cruz con Cristo vendrá.

9

The cross is held in escrow,
And the host is deep within,
And at the final judgment,
The cross with Christ will be seen.

9

Adoremos a Jesús,
todos postrados al suelo,
y la Santísima Cruz,
abrirá las puertas del cielo.

10

Let us adore you, our sweet Jesus,
All prostrate on the floor,
And the most holy cross
Will open the heavenly doors.

10

Si todo esto me concede,
yo te doy el parabién,
con la Santísima Cruz
en fin diagamos: amén.

11

If this he does bestow on me,
I will bid you all farewell,
With the most holy cross,
We will say in the end: amen.

11

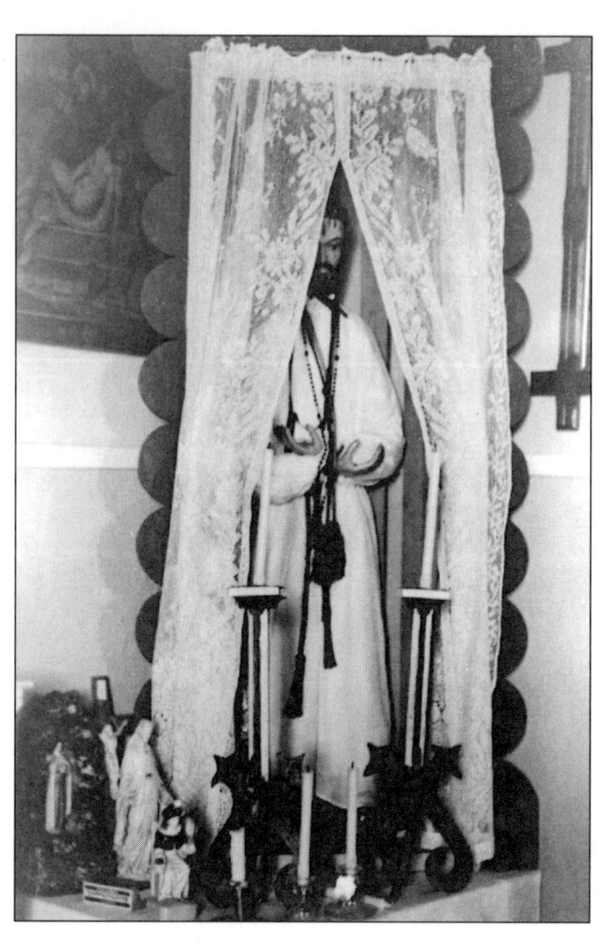

Nuestro Padre Jesús *(Our Father Jesus). Taos, New Mexico. Courtesy Kit Carson Museum Foundation.*

✝ 18 ✝

POR SER MI DIVINA LUZ
YOU ARE MY DIVINE LIGHT

This hymn is primarily an exhortation to the sinner to pay homage to Our Lord and to abide by his law, especially in view of the great sufferings he endured during the Passion.

Por ser mi divina luz,	You are my divine light,
¡Ay! Jesús del alma mía,	Oh, Jesus of my soul,
llevando en mi compañía	Taking into my company
a nuestro Padre Jesús.	Our Father Jesus Christ.
1	1
Escuchen bien, pecadores,	Listen well, sinners,
los esclavos de Jesús,	All you slaves of Jesus Christ,
cumplan con el juramento	Comply with your oath to
de nuestro Padre Jesús.	Our Father Jesus Christ.
2	2
Hoy aclamemos, los cofrados,	Today we proclaim, my brothers,
hoy aclamemos esa luz,	Today we proclaim your light,
para llevar en el pecho	So that I may take into my soul
a nuestro Padre Jesús.	Our Father Jesus Christ.
3	3
Oiganme bien pecadores	Listen well, sinners,
y veneren esta luz	And venerate this light,
que es la llaga del costado	Which is the wound in the side
de nuestro Padre Jesús.	Of our Father Jesus Christ.
4	4

Oiganme bien, pecadores
y contemplen esta luz
que es la divina corona
de nuestro Padre Jesús.

5

Pecadores, pecadores,
que padecen por Jesús
hoy veneremos los clavos
de nuestro Padre Jesús.

6

En los brazos lo estrechamos,
aquí esta divina luz
para contemplar las llagas
de nuestro Padre Jesús.

7

Los esclavos que veneran
aquí, esta divina luz
en su compañía lleven
a nuestro Padre Jesús.

8

Hermanos, los verdaderos,
acompañen a Jesús,
no quebranten el misterio
de nuestro Padre Jesús.

9

Felices los que contemplan
en su sagrada pasión,
y que reciben su cuerpo
en la Santa Comunión.

10

Listen well, sinners,
And contemplate this light,
Which is the divine crown
Of our Father Jesus Christ.

5

Sinners, sinners,
Who suffer for Jesus Christ,
Today we venerate the nails
Of our Father Jesus Christ.

6

In our arms we embrace it,
Here is the divine light,
To contemplate the wounds
Of our Father Jesus Christ.

7

The slaves who come here
To venerate this divine light,
Into their company will take
Our Father Jesus Christ.

8

Brothers, those who truly believe,
Follow Jesus Christ,
Do not turn away from the mystery
Of our Father Jesus Christ.

9

Happy are those who contemplate
Your sacred passion
And receive your body
In Holy Communion.

10

Los que creen en la cruz
y en esta divina luz,
son esclavos verdaderos
de nuestro Padre Jesús.

11

Vamos todos de rodillas,
adorando aquí esta luz,
con un credo y una salve
a nuestro Padre Jesús.

12

Those who believe in the cross
And in this divine light
Are true slaves
Of our Father Jesus Christ.

11

Let us all get on our knees,
Adoring here this light,
With a creed and a prayer
To our Father Jesus Christ.

12

Nuestra Señora de San Juan de Los Lagos *(Our Lady of St. John of the Lakes), by J. Guadalupe Góngora. Nineteenth-century engraving, Mexico. De Aragón family collection.*

✝ 19 ✝

Venid, Venid, Señor Mío
Come, Come, My Dear Lord Jesus

Los Hermanos de la Luz are called upon to intone this long and emotional narrative of Christ's Passion. This alabado, which expresses deep devotion to Mary, mother of Christ, concludes with a series of farewells that signal the end of the observation of the Passion. Stanza 44, which mentions the shedding of blood, is of particular interest.

Los Hermanos de Sangre (Brothers of Blood) was the flagellant group of the Brotherhood. In the procession, they followed the crossbearers and the Brother pulling the death cart. A matraca (a ratcheted wooden rattle), a flute, and sometimes a drum were the instruments used to accompany the measured verses and rhythmic penitential movements of the participants. With their bowed heads covered by short black hoods to demonstrate their humility, the Brothers arched their bare backs and commenced their penance. In rows of two, three, or more, depending on the number participating, they would take three steps in cadence, then stop at the end of each verse and swing the disciplina (a whip plaited from strips of the fibrous amole plant) over one shoulder. If they stopped with the right foot forward, they would swing the disciplina over the left shoulder, then they would proceed three more steps, stop at the end of the next verse with the left foot forward, and swing the disciplina over the right shoulder. Their self-flagellation would continue until the alabado was sung to the end and would start up again when the next alabado began.

All of the penitential devotions had a set structure. The penances included binding cactus to one's body with *mecates* (horsehair or cotton cords), walking on knees over rough terrain, having one's outstretched arms bound for a short period to a crossbeam of a cross at the Calvario (the proxy for Mount Calvary, often situated at the top of a hill or rise), and lying near a church entrance face down and being stepped on by the faithful.

The Brothers also used *Venid, venid, Señor mío* to perform their self-flagellation ceremony within the confines of the morada. Each would kneel down, sometimes bare kneed, on fine flinty pebbles gathered from anthills and would rhythmically swing his whip over one shoulder at the end of a stanza, pull it down and hold still, then swing it over the other shoulder at the end of the next stanza, continuing thusly until the end of the recitation.

Venid, venid, Señor mío, *en el santo sacramento,* *adorar la santa cruz* *de mi Jesús Nazareno.*	Come, come to me, Lord Jesus, In the Holy Sacrament, I praise you on your holy cross, Jesus, for what you did for us.
1	1
El miércoles de pasión, *el primer día que es cierto* *el padecimiento santo* *de mi Jesús Nazareno.*	Wednesday of Holy Week We are sure is the first day Of the most holy suffering Of Jesus of Nazareth.
2	2
¡Oh, divino corazón! *¡Oh, dichosa sangre vio!* *Que derramó Jesucristo* *cuando al calvario llegó.*	Oh, divine heart! Oh, divine blood flowing! Shed by our savior Jesus Christ While to Calvary he was going.
3	3

Hoy tienen cristianos todos,
pues el santo sacramento,
la sangre de mi Jesús,
pues viene regando el suelo.

Now all Christendom is sharing
The most blessed sacrament,
While the blood of Christ is flowing
A cause for our lament.

4

Hermosa sangre amorosa,
árbol de la santa cruz,
pues con sangre y cruz
viene ya el dulce Jesús.

4

Oh, precious, loving blood,
Tree of the holy cross,
With this cross and flowing blood
Comes our sweet Jesus.

5

Dulce Padre de mi vida,
dulce Jesús infinito,
porque aquí está derramada
la sangre de Jesucristo.

5

Sweet Father of my life,
Sweet Jesus most infinite,
For here is where you spilled
The blood of Jesus Christ.

6

Aquí me tienes postrado
a tus pies dulce Jesús,
suspirando por tu amor
al pie de la santa cruz.

6

Here you have me prostrate
At your feet, my sweet Jesus,
Yearning for your precious love
At the foot of your holy cross.

7

¡Oh, divino Padre amado!
¡Oh, divino Hijo Jesús!
Te vemos enarbolado
y reacostado en la cruz.

7

Oh, divine loving God!
Oh, divine Son Jesus!
We see you hanging
And stretched out on the cross.

8

Cruel corona le pusieron
los judíos como se ha visto,
para que contemplen todos
la sangre de Jesucristo.

8

Cruel crown of thorns they placed
On Jesus, as we know,
So that we could contemplate
The blood of Jesus Christ.

9

9

"Hijo," le dice María
con palabras de dolor,
"Pues ya vas a padecer,
por salvar al pecador."

"Son," said Mary,
With words of so much caring,
"Soon you will die
To save the sinner."

10

Las cinco llagas mortales,
que tu cuerpo recibió;
tu sangre fue derramada
cuando al Calvario llegó.

The five mortal wounds
That your body received,
The blood that you shed
When you reached Calvary.

11

El amantísimo velo
con que vendaron tu cara
y aquella cuerda y cilicio
con que verdugos le daban.

That lifting veil
Bound over your face
And that rope and hair shirt
Were a terrible disgrace.

12

Oh, amantísimo nombre
que en Roma lo habían visto,
en aquel monte Calvario
donde mofaron a Cristo.

Oh, most holy name
That was heard far off in Rome,
It was on Mount Calvary
That they gave you a home.

13

Si vemos aquí los clavos
con que en la cruz lo clavaron
a mi amantísimo Dios
y su sangre blasfemaron.

We can see the nails
That were used to crucify
My most holy Father,
And his blood was blasphemed.

14

Y coronaron las sienes del
Dios eterno infinito,
y blasfemaron su sangre
del divino Jesucristo.

And they crowned the temples
Of our eternal and infinite God,
And they blasphemed the blood
Of my most divine Jesus Christ.

15

Y lo ponen en la cruz
para empezarlo a burlar,
la sangre de Jesucristo
vendremos a contemplar.

16

Venid, venid, pecadores,
venid, venid, adorar,
la pasión de Jesucristo
que lo van a tormentar.

17

Padre celestial del cielo,
que coronado te vemos,
la sangre de Jesucristo
pues ahora contemplemos.

18

Y renegrido el color,
que en su rostro se ha visto,
en su bendita pasión,
la sangre de Jesucristo.

19

Aquí va ya caminando
con aquel tormento triste,
por la calle más amarga,
pasearon a Jesucristo.

20

Los Fariseos lo tomaron
y le dan con cruel cilicio,
para derramar la sangre
del divino Jesucristo.

21

And they placed him on the cross
To continue their defamation,
Of Jesus' blood so precious
We continue our contemplation.

16

Come, come, sinners,
Come, come, in adoration,
The passion of our Redeemer,
They continue his persecution.

17

Celestial Father up above,
We see your coronation,
You shed your blood for us,
We continue our contemplation.

18

And scarlet is the color
That covered his holy face,
In his most holy passion,
The blood of Jesus Christ.

19

Through here he travels slowly
With a most sorrowful affliction,
Through the street so painfully,
Jesus Christ in persecution.

20

The Pharisees take him
And scourge him without hesitation
To spill the precious blood
Of our divine Jesus Christ.

21

Vamos a adorar, hermanos,	Let us adore, my brothers,
la aflicción que aquí vemos,	The affliction we are seeing,
para contemplar	So that we may contemplate with
con ella,	Mary
la sangre de Jesucristo.	The blood of Jesus Christ.
22	22
De púrpura manto lleva,	He is wearing the purple mantle,
la vestidura sagrada	The most sacred vestment
con su sangre teñida,	Stained with his blood,
la cruz está enarbolada.	While the cross awaits his hanging.
23	23
De dolor queda oprimida,	They tyrannize her with pain,
la dulcísima María,	Most sweet and gentle Mary,
de ver a su Hijo en la cruz,	Pain from seeing her son on the cross
el viernes al medio día.	At noon on Good Friday.
24	24
Y con dolor de amargura	And with pain so bitter,
adora la cruz que ha visto	She adores the cross she has seen
y contemplamos en ella,	And we contemplate in her,
la sangre de Jesucristo.	The blood of Jesus Christ.
25	25
Todos vamos de rodillas,	We all travel on our knees,
con nuestra madre llorando,	Crying with our Mother,
la sangre de Jesucristo,	Well, let us contemplate
pues vámosla contemplando.	The blood of Jesus Christ.
26	26
En aquel monte Calvario,	On his way to Mount Calvary,
la Verónica lo ha visto	Veronica has seen him,
y con un lienzo le limpia,	And with a cloth she cleaned
la sangre y rostro a Cristo.	The bloody face of Christ.
27	27

Aquí mi Dios verdadero,
mi Jesús dulce infinito,
a quien vimos derramar,
la sangre de Jesucristo.

28

Aquí tenemos hermanos,
aquí este sello divino,
de los que recibió,
nuestra Madre por su Hijo.

29

Que dolor tan excesivo,
aquí su madre ha visto,
haciendo comer su sangre,
le limpió el sudor a Cristo.

30

Cristo, a la Virgen le dice,
"¡Ay Madre de mis entrañas,
aquí va morir tu Hijo,
para salvar las almas todas!"

31

Va gimiendo y suspirando,
en tan terrible batalla,
va derramando su sangre,
por librarnos de las llamas.

32

Ese fuego tenebroso,
que en el infierno se ha visto
se apaciguaron las llamas,
viendo la sangre de Cristo.

33

Here is my God of truth,
My sweet infinite Jesus,
Whom we saw suffer,
The blood of Jesus Christ.

28

Here we have it, brothers,
Here is the divine seal,
Which was received
By our Mother for her son.

29

The pain was so excessive,
Here his mother saw,
His bleeding so extravagant,
She cleaned the brow of Christ.

30

Christ to his mother proclaimed,
"Oh, Mother of my humility,
Here your son will die
To save the souls of humanity!"

31

He continues moaning and sighing,
In such terrible lamentation,
Spilling his precious blood
To liberate us from damnation.

32

The flames of the eternal fire
That we know in Hell exists
Were soothed and pacified
Upon seeing the blood of Christ.

33

¿Dime, Padre de mi vida,
al tomar este cilicio,
si ha de ser mi salvación,
tomar la sangre de Cristo?

Tell me, Father of my life,
As I subject myself to mortification,
As I take the blood of Christ,
Will this be my salvation?

34

¡Ay! Jesús grande, clemente,
Jesús que fuerte suspiro,
aquí adoremos la muerte
de nuestro Padre Jesús.

Oh, great merciful Jesus!
Jesus what a great gasp,
Here we adore the death
Of our Father Jesus Christ.

35

Gruesas cadenas le ponen,
en su divina garganta
con esos crueles cilicios
que a su cuerpo le quebrantan.

Heavy chains were placed,
Around his divine throat,
They dressed him in cruel haircloth
To defile his body.

36

"Con aquel inmenso amor,
cuando se vio en el sepulcro
el Hijo de mis entrañas,
estaba salvando al mundo."

"With such immense affection,
When he found himself entombed,
The son of my soul
Was saving the world."

37

Dulce madre de mi vida,
la petición que a tu Hijo
y con sus dulces clavos
y valiéndose del suplicio.

Sweet Mother of my life,
Please give him my petition,
And through his dying on the cross,
He granted my remission.

38

Aquieta dulce Jesús,
el pecado que siguió,
reclamando ya su sello,
el viernes en que dio.

Remove sweet Jesus,
The sin that followed,
Reclaim the seal you earned,
On the Friday on which you died.

39

¡Adiós, mi divina madre!
¡Adiós, dichoso manjar!
La sangre de Jesucristo,
allí se queda en el altar.

Goodbye, my divine Mother!
Goodbye, blessed nourishment!
The blood of Jesus Christ,
Remains on the altar.

40

¡Adiós, divina esperanza!
¡Adiós, divino consuelo!
La sangre de Jesucristo,
hoy se queda en este suelo.

Goodbye, divine hope!
Goodbye, divine consolation!
The blood of Jesus Christ
Today will remain on the ground.

41

¡Adiós, divino Jesús!
¡Adiós, dulcísimo canto!
¡Adiós, hostia consagrada!
¡Adiós, Espíritu Santo!

Goodbye, divine Jesus!
Goodbye, most sweet song!
Goodbye, consecrated host!
Goodbye, Holy Spirit!

42

Ya voy a acabar Señora,
de cantar esta pasión,
que padeció Jesucristo,
por salvar al pecador.

I am coming to the end, dear lady,
In singing of this passion,
How our Lord died on the cross
For the sinners' salvation.

43

¡Adiós, toditas las almas!
¡Adiós, almas de mi vida!
Allí se les queda mi sangre,
hoy se llegó mi partida.

Goodbye, all holy spirits!
Goodbye, spirits of my salvation!
Here I will leave my blood,
Today I will depart.

44

¡Adiós, mi querida madre!
¡Adiós, todo mi consuelo!
¡Adiós, mi querido Padre!
¡Adiós, ángeles del cielo!

Goodbye, my beloved Mother!
Goodbye, my consolation!
Goodbye, my most loving Father!
Goodbye, angels of exaltation!

45

¡Adiós, ángeles benditos!
¡Adiós, todos los santos!
¡Adiós, el cáliz precioso!
¡Adiós, dulcísimo
encanto!

46

Goodbye, angels of benediction!
Goodbye, saints of encouragement!
Goodbye, chalice of inspiration!
Goodbye, my most sweet
enchantment!

46

¡Adiós, dulcísima madre!
¡Adiós, mi amparo y mi guía!
¡Adiós, la sangre de Cristo!
¡Adiós, por último día!

47

Goodbye, my most sweet Mother!
Goodbye, my light and guide!
Goodbye, the blood of Christ!
Goodbye, on the last day!

47

A las llagas amorosas,
que Jesucristo tenía,
¡Adiós, el padecimiento!
¡Adiós, Jesús de mi vida!

48

To the amorous wounds
That Jesus Christ endured,
Goodbye to affliction!
Goodbye, Jesus of my life!

48

A las llagas amorosas,
que Jesucristo tenía.
¡Adiós, el padecimiento!
¡Adiós, Jesús de mi vida!

49

To the amorous wounds
That Jesus Christ endured,
Goodbye to affliction!
Goodbye, Jesus of my life!

49

✝ 20 ✝

Ayudemos, Almas
Please Help Us, Poor Souls

In this beautifully harmonious alabado, which was sung after the recitation of the rosary on the evening of Good Friday, the congregation is entreated to join with Our Lady of Solitude during the most grievous hours of the Passion of her son. The alabado consists of quatrains in which the second and fourth lines rhyme.

Ayudemos, almas,	Please help us poor souls,
de tanto penar	To dispel the worry
a la Virgen pura	Of the pure Virgin
de la Soledad.	Of Solitude, Mary.
1	1
Al pie de la cruz	At the foot of the cross
la vemos que estaba	We saw that she was
la Madre sin Hijo	A mother without a son
porque ha muerto ya.	Because he had been taken from her.
2	2
Se aumenta su pena	Augmented is her sorrow
de ver a Jesús,	Upon seeing Jesus,
que no hay quien lo baje	There is no one to lower
de la Santa Cruz.	Him from the holy cross.
3	3
Crece su dolor,	The pain pierced her heart
pues no hallan sudario	As they searched for a cloth
para revestir	To find a pure vestment
el cuerpo sagrado.	For her sacred son.
4	4

Tanta es su pobreza,
pues no hayan sepulcro
para sepultar
a su Hijo difunto.

5

Tres necesidades
tuvo esta Señora,
pero Dios le envió
quien se las socorra.

6

José y Nicodemos
de Arimatea
bajan a Jesús
y a María lo entregan.

7

Con sus dülces brazos
tierno lo estrechaba
con amargo llanto
sus llagas besaba.

8

"¡Ay, Hijo de mi alma,
prenda de mi vida,
cómo está t
u cuerpo
todo hecho una herida!

9

"Por culpas ajenas
estas de esta suerte,
por librar al hombre
de la eterna muerte."

10

So great is her poverty,
No tomb could she buy
To bury our Savior,
Whom she watched die.

5

Three great needs
Our Lady had to endure,
But our loving God leads
Someone to assist her.

6

Joseph and Nicodemus
Of Arimathea
Lowered our Lord Jesus
And turned him over to Mary.

7

With her sweet arms
She embraced him tenderly,
With painful weeping
She kissed his wounds.

8

"Oh, Son of my pierced heart,
Jewel of my salvation,
Your body covered through
every part
With cruel wounds of affliction.

9

"For other people's crimes
You came to this condition,
To keep the world this time
From eternal condemnation."

10

Sepulcro a Jesús
dieron, a su Madre
de pena y dolor
el pecho se le abre.

11

Con San Juan se va
porque es el amado
a quien Jesucristo
la habia encomendado.

12

Allí vio la calle
donde le prendieron
y donde de muerte
sentencia le dieron.

13

Triste y afligida,
entra a la ciudad,
llena de dolor,
llena de pesar.

14

Entra a su aposento,
se desata en llanto,
no hay quien la consuele
en tanto quebranto.

15

Hombre, fuiste causa
de esta soledad,
llora tu pecado,
llora tu maldad.

16

A tomb to Jesus
They gave, to his mother
Pain and sorrow,
Her heart was pierced.

11

With Saint John she left,
Because he was the one
Jesus Christ had said
Would be her only son.

12

There she viewed the path
Where he had been arrested
And upon which the death
Sentence was given.

13

Sad and filled with grief,
She entered the city,
Filled with pain,
Completely mortified.

14

She entered her abode,
Overtaken with distress,
No one could console her
In her crushing grief.

15

Mankind was the cause
Of all this solitude,
Cry for your sin,
Cry for your ingratitude.

16

Herido tu pecho	Wounded is your heart
con siete puñales	With seven swords
tus ojos en llanto,	Your eyes weeping,
Señora te deshaces.	Our Lady of Sorrows.
17	17
"¿Dónde está mi amado?"	"Where is my beloved son?"
decía adolorida.	She said in tears.
"¿Dónde está mi bien?	"Where is happiness?
¿Dónde está mi vida?"	Where shall I go from here?"
18	18
¡Salve, dolorosa,	Hail, Mother of Sorrows,
afligida Madre!	Mother of affliction!
¡Salve, tus dolores,	Hail to your pain,
a todos nos	Which you suffered for our
salve!	salvation!
19	19
¡Adiós, Madre Mía!	Goodbye, my dear Mother!
¡Adiós, mi consuelo!	Goodbye, my consolation!
¡Adiós, mi esperanza!	Goodbye, my hope!
¡Adiós, mi remedio!	Goodbye, my source of restoration!
20	20

✝ 21 ✝
LA ENCOMENDACIÓN DEL ALMA
THE COMMENDING OF THE SOUL

La Encomendación del alma is one of a group of alabados sung during the wake of a departed Brother. A three-day wake was held at the Brother's home or at the morada if it was located near the village. The Brothers chanted alabados and prayed each night. The corpse was taken outside of the house on the final night and laid on a wooden table and *La Encomendación del alma* was sung. Several Brothers whipped themselves at the end of each stanza as they moved around the body to atone for their deceased brother's sins. The entire ceremony lasted about half an hour. At its conclusion, the body was brought back inside and the rosary was recited at midnight. A meal was shared at the end of the wake. El Hermano Mayor sang *Adios al mundo* (Goodbye to the World) at the burial site the next day.

La Encomendación del alma is highly significant because it provides an important clue as to the origins of the Brotherhood. Stanza 10 reads,

Oh San Vicente amoroso,	O loving St. Vincent,
pues tú anunciaste la luz,	Well, you announced the light,
llévate esta alma con gozo,	Take this soul with joy
y entrégasela a Jesús.	And deliver it to Jesus.

Since there were several St. Vincents, including St. Vincent Ferrer and St. Vincent de Paul, it is open to question which one is being referred to. Further investigation suggests Vincent Ferrer is meant, since he was recognized as the penitent saint. St. Vincent Ferrer is described as the "benign father," implored as the "Protector," and credited as the mentor of the Brotherhood in several hymns. These include *San Vincente, Protector* (St. Vincent, Protector), *Alegre Cantemos* (Happy We Sing), *Celebramos la gloria* (We Celebrate the Glory), and *¡O! Sed del alto cielo* (Oh, You from Heaven High). If St. Vincent Ferrer was the progenitor of the Brotherhood, then this would explain the similarity between the ideas, beliefs, and practices of the Penitentes in New Mexico and those promulgated by the saint. *La Encomendación del alma* may help resolve this issue.

The following is from the Pecos Cuaderno:

La Encomendación del alma	The commending of the soul
no la dejes de pedir,	One should not stop asking for,
encomiéndasela a Dios	Entrust it to God
que Dios la ha de recibir.	So that God may receive it.
1	1
Oh divino Redentor	O divine Redeemer,
hijo del eterno padre,	Son of the eternal Father,
a ti te encomiendo esa alma	To you I commend that soul
que la cuides, que se salve.	That it may be taken care of and saved.
2	2
Santísimo sacramento	Most holy Sacrament
que la hostia reciviste,	The host you received,
a ti te encomiendo esa alma	To you I commend that soul
que la lleves a tu reino.	That you will carry to its glory.
3	3

Oh Jesús divino querido
hijo de José y María,
recibe esta alma en tus brazos
y téngala en tu compañia.

4

Oh madre de mi Señor
madre de los pecadores,
recibe esta alma en tu reino
atienda a nuestros clamores.

5

Misericordia Señor,
te pido y vuelvo a rogar,
que lleves esta alma a la gloria,
la lleves a descansar.

6

Ya con humildad te pido,
que esta alma tenga consuelo,
y llévala a descansar,
siquiera al último seno.

7

Oh sangre de mi Jesús,
oh remedio universal,
llévate esta alma a tu gloria
no la dejes estrabiar.

8

Sangre dulce y afable,
fuiste de María esposo,
llévate esta alma a los cielos
llévala lleno de gozo.

9

O divine Jesus, beloved
Son of Joseph and Mary,
Receive this soul in your arms
And keep it in your company.

4

O Mother of my Lord,
Mother of all sinners,
Receive this soul in your kingdom,
Attend to our pleadings.

5

Merciful Lord,
I ask and I beg
That you carry this soul to glory,
That you carry it to its rest.

6

With humility I ask of you
That this soul have consolation
And be carried to its rest,
At least to the final womb.

7

O blood of my Jesus,
Universal remedy,
Carry this soul to your glory,
Don't let it stray away.

8

Blood so sweet and pleasant,
You were Mary's husband,
Carry this soul to the heavens,
Carry it with much joy.

9

Oh San Vicente amoroso, *pues tu anunciaste la luz,* *llévate esta alma con gozo,* *y entrégasela a Jesús.*	O loving St. Vincent, You announced the light, Carry this soul with joy, And deliver it to Jesus.
10	10
Oh Virgen madre de Dios, *madre Mía y abogada,* *ruégale a tu hijo divino,* *que esta alma sea perdonada.*	O Virgin Mother of God, My Mother and intercessor, Pray to your divine son, So that this soul will be forgiven.
11	11
Ruégale madre amorosa, *yo te ruego madre amada,* *que vaya esta alma a los cielos,* *de ángeles acompañada.*	Pray, O loving Mother, I beg of you, beloved Mother, That this soul may go to the heavens Accompanied by angels.
12	12
Ángeles y querubines, *que la vengan a topar,* *que la lleven a los cielos,* *que de Dios vaya a gozar.*	Angels and cherubim, That they come to meet it, That they may carry it to the heavens, To find joy with God.
13	13
Santo Niñito de Atocha, *pastorcito de tus ovejas,* *junta esta alma en tu rebaño,* *y perdónale sus quejas.*	Holy Infant of Atocha, Little pastor of your sheep, Accept this soul into your flock And pardon its lament.
14	14
Oh Dios mió omnipotente, *Padre, Hijo, Espíritu Santo,* *llévate esta alma a los cielos* *a que cante "Oh Santo, Santo."*	O my God omnipotent, Father, Son, and Holy Spirit, Take this soul to the heavens, That it may sing "O Holy, Holy."
15	15

Llévasela a cantarle santo
a esa hermosa claridad,
con ángeles y querubines,
y toda la santidad.

16

Oh divino Redentor,
oh Virgen y madre querida,
yo te recomiendo esa alma,
que sea bien recibida.

17

Rogándole estoy Señor,
y todos los santos tambíen,
que la lleves a los cielos,
por los siglos de los siglos.

18

Take it to sing most sacred,
In beautiful clarity,
With angels and cherubim
And all the holy saints.

16

O divine Redeemer,
O Virgin and beloved Mother,
I recommend that soul
May be well received.

17

Praying I am, O Lord,
And all of the saints also,
That you carry it to the heavens,
Forever and ever.

18

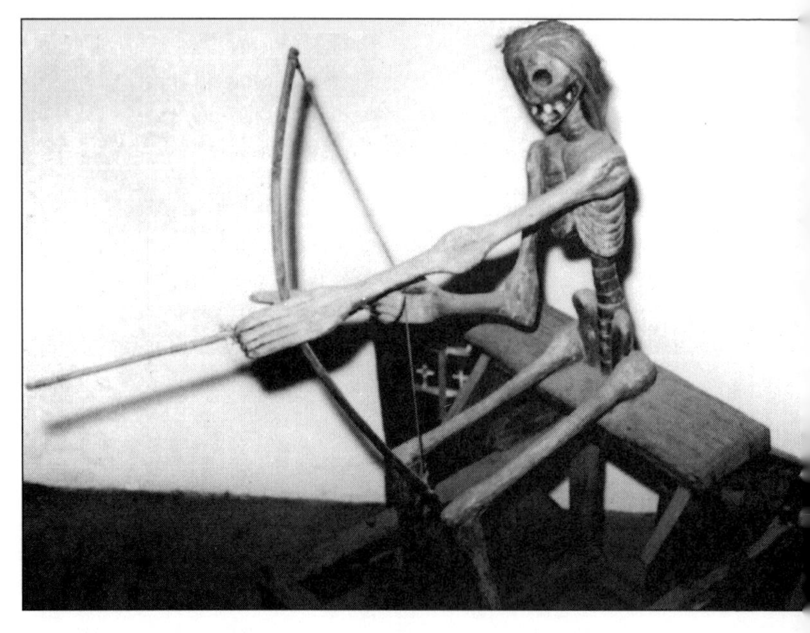

Carreta de la muerte *(Penitente death cart). Nineteenth-century, Taos, New Mexico. Courtesy Kit Carson Museum Foundation.*

✝ 22 ✝

ACUERDATE MORTAL
REMEMBER MORTAL

The use of an animated skeleton to represent death has been preserved in New Mexico by the Penitentes. Death is familiarly called *Doña Sebastiana* (Venerable Lady), *La Comadre Sebastiana* (The Venerable Friend), or simply *La Muerte* (Death). The death image is a carved wooden skeleton with protruding ribs, gray or white horsehair or a human hair wig, and obsidian, mica, or hollow eyes, and it either is toothless or has human teeth. In some cases, death is represented holding an axe or hatchet but more commonly is shown with a drawn bow and arrow. Death is sometimes clothed in a black dress and a black hood and is usually seated in a *carreta de la muerte* (death cart).

The terrifying portrayals of death in New Mexico trace their origins to artistic representations of death created during the Middle Ages. In a woodcut from *Der Ackermann aus Bohmen* (The Ploughman from Bohemia), we find death as a skeleton with drawn bow and arrow riding on a horse. In a 1482 engraving by Master H. W. (Wolf Hammer), death is shown flinging arrows at unsuspecting victims. In a woodblock print from Geiler von Kaisersperg's sermons, *De arbore humana,* printed by Johann Gruninger in 1514, death appears not only with a drawn bow but with an axe in its belt.

The small Penitente death carts almost always closely resembled the wooden supply carts brought into the New World by the Spanish conquistadors, explorers, and settlers. Slight variations were introduced, depending on the needs of the area and the availability of the materials. Some of the larger death carts were pulled in the penitential processions. Typically, a partially nude Brother would pull the cart using a horsehair rope that was passed over his bare shoulders and under his arms. Sometimes the penance of pulling the cart was made more difficult by adding rocks to the cart or jamming the wheels to make them drag on the ground.

The following alabado, *Acuérdate mortal*, which was sung in the presence of La Muerte, affirms the importance of heeding the fact that death is ever near. With the imminence of death in mind, the Penitentes concluded their holy services by singing farewells to Christ, his blessed mother, and the saints.

Acuérdate, mortal,
el fin fatal
del sepulcro el horror
do te encaminas:
contempla con temor;
así sólo sabrás
aprovechar la vida.
Hombres, debéis morir,
debéis morir;
pensad en bien vivir;
debéis morir,
pensad en bien vivir.

1

Riqueza, dignidad,
es vanidad
tu falaz pompa:
todo viene a parar,
¡Cuán amargo pesar!

Remember, mortal,
The fatal end
The tomb and the horror
Toward which you are traveling:
Contemplate and tremble;
That way you will know how to
profit from life.
Men, you will die,
You will die;
Think of being good;
You will die,
Think of being good.

1

Riches, dignity,
It's all vanity,
Your fraudulent pomp:
All will come to an end,
Oh what bitter grief!

En la estrecha mansión del
féretro sombrío.

2

Gracia y saber,
inexorable,
en gusano y fetor,
en cenizas y horro
cambias, muerte cruel, sin
que a nadie perdones.

3

Como ladrón vendrás,
nos quitarás
amigos, bienes:
disipara el error
tu lúgubre fulgor:
oh muerte, tu lección ¡cuan
recta y saludable!

4

¿Pues hemos de morir
por qué vivir
con tanto apego
a este cuerpo mortal,
mísero y criminal?
tratemos de salvar a nuestra
alma inmortal.

5

Piénsalo pecador:
con qué pavor
en aquel día
tu locura verás,
y como acabarás

In the brief journey of the darkened
hearse.

2

Grace and knowledge,
Relentless,
In worm and stench,
In ashes and horror,
You will change, cruel death,
without forgiving anyone.

3

Like a thief you will come,
You will take away
Friends, material wealth:
Error will be dispelled
By your dismal brilliance:
Oh death, your lesson, how just
and salubrious!

4

Well, we have to die,
Why live
With such attachment
To this mortal body,
Miserable and criminal?
Let us try to save our soul,
which is immortal.

5

Think about it sinner:
With what terror
On that day
Your madness you will see,
And how will you end

¡Tu vida criminal con desdichada muerte!

6

Más el fiel servidor
de su Señor
en El espera;
con suave sumisión
paz y consolación,
al mundo dejarás por gozar de la vida.

7

Soberano Hacedor,
justo Señor,
que castigaste
al hombre criminal
con la muerte fatal.
Tu fallo divinal adoramos sumisos.

8

Santos haznos vivir,
siempre vivir
en tu gracia y morir;
siempre vivir
en tu gracia y morir.

9

Your criminal life with a calamitous death!

6

Moreover, the faithful servant
Of the Lord,
On him he waits;
With soft submission,
Peace and contemplation,
The world you will leave to enjoy life.

7

Sovereign Maker
Just Lord,
Who punished
Criminal man
With ominous death,
To your divine judgment adoringly we submit.

8

Help us to be holy,
To always live
In your grace and die;
To always live
In your grace and die.

9

✟ 23 ✟
SALVE VIRGEN PURA
HAIL, VIRGIN, OH MOST PURE

In contrast to their male counterparts, the Carmelitas have received virtually no attention in the historical literature. This may be due in part to the fact that the Hermanos were sensationalized by the media because of the practice of self-flagellation.

The origins of the penitential order of the Carmelitas are similar to those of the Brotherhood. The devotees commemorate an incident in the life of St. Simon Stock. Born in the county of Kent around 1165, St. Simon Stock was a prior general of the Carmelite Order at Aylesford. He aided in the growth of the order and constantly invoked the Blessed Mother with a prayer he wrote entitled *Flos Carmel*. It is stated that the holy friar witnessed an apparition of the Virgin Mary at Aylesford in 1251. During the appearance, the Virgin Mary promised special graces to all those who would wear the brown scapular of the Carmelite habit in her honor. The Carmelitas, in their devotion to Mary, wore the scapular, observed days of abstinence each week, offered prayers, sang praises to her, and performed works of mercy.

The devotion to Our Lady of Mount Carmel can be traced back to the prophet Elias' vision of a white cloud rising toward the heavens at Mount Carmel in Palestine. The white cloud, which apparently was later interpreted as a white dove, was taken to represent the Mother of Christ.

In New Mexico both the Hermanos de la Luz ("Brothers of the Light of Christ" is used to identify the Penitentes collectively as followers of Christ) and the Carmelitas were devoted to *Nuestra Señora del Carmen* (Our Lady of Mount Carmel). Her scapular was regarded as their shield against all sin. The portrayal of Nuestra Señora del Carmen was very popular with the santeros, and the adoration for her among the people was so intense that they were buried with the Carmelite scapular, as some of the Penitente hymns illustrate.

The Carmelitas took their membership in their penitential association as seriously as the men took theirs. Among other tasks, they prepared meals that the Brothers carried with them to the moradas during their Lenten observances. They produced the embroidered altar cloths for the Penitente altars and church altars. They manufactured the clothing used to dress the santos for religious ceremonies and, on occasion, helped the santeros paint the holy images. They made ramilletes (paper flowers dipped in wax) and other decorations for the altars. In essence, women toiled in the background, serving as the backbone of their families and preserving Spanish culture, language, traditions, faith, and family values. It is possible the women even wrote some of the alabados.

The Carmelitas performed their own acts of penance. At times they wore prickly horsehair girdles under their outer garments, causing severe pain and discomfort. They often wore long black dresses and *tapalos* (shawls), not only as a symbol of the sorrowful Mother of Christ but often because they were mourning the loss of a husband, child, or relative. They whipped the flesh of their backs privately with *cuerdas* (braided cords) and spent long hours in prayer and devotion; singing hymns like the following:

Salve, Virgen pura
salve, Virgen Madre,
salve, Virgen bella
reina Virgen, salve.

1

Gózate, María,
patrona del Carmen,
con las alabanzas
de estos tus cofrades.

2

Vuestro amparo buscan
benigno y suave
hoy los desterrados
en aqueste valle.

3

Eres del Carmelo
la pastora amable,
que a tus ovejuelas
das pastro suave.

4

A ti pues, clamamos
buscando piedades;
¡Ea! pues, Señora,
no nos desampares.

5

Es tu escapulario
la cadena grande,
con que se aprisiona
el dragón infame.

6

Hail, Virgin, O most pure,
Hail, Virgin Mother,
Hail, beautiful Virgin,
Queenly Virgin, hail.

1

Rejoice, Mary,
Patroness of Carmel,
With these praises that are coming
From your members' pleading.

2

All seeking your protection,
Merciful and soft,
Today are the exiles
Of this valley calling.

3

You are of Carmel
The pleasing shepherdess,
That to your sheep
Gives merciful nourishment.

4

To you we cry,
Seeking your compassion;
Well then, Our Lady,
Please don't desert us.

5

Your scapular is
The mighty mighty chain
That certainly imprisons
The infamous dragon.

6

Volved a nosotros,
oh piadosa Madre,
esos vuestros ojos
llenos de piedades.

7

Por ti defendidos
viven tus cofrades
libres de peligros
y de todos males.

8

Muéstranos, María,
benigna y afable
de tu puro vientre
el fruto admirable.

9

Es contra el infierno
tu poder tan grande,
que libras a las almas
de eternos volcanes.

10

Si por nuestra culpa
penas a millares
merecemos todos,
tu favor nos salve.

11

Si al Purgatorio
bajan tus cofrades,
pedimos, Señora,
que al punto los saques.

12

Turn back to us,
O pious Mother Mary,
Those eyes of yours
So full of godliness.

7

Through your defense
Live your association members,
Free of danger
And everything that's bad.

8

Show us, oh Mother Mary,
Merciful and kind,
From your womb most pure
Comes the admirable fruit.

9

Against all Hell's inferno
Your power is so great
That you liberate the souls
From the eternal flames.

10

O merciful, O holy
Never failing fountain,
Where are refreshed
All of humankind.

11

If to Purgatory
We should descend,
Pray for us, Sweet Lady,
That we may join you in Heaven.

12

Oh clemente, oh pia,
fuente inagotable,
do se refrigeran
todos los mortales.

O clement, o pious
Fountain unending,
Where are refreshed
All of mankind.

13

Salve Virgen pura,
rosa muy fragante,
flor que de la vida
con olor tan suave.

Hail, Virgin, oh most pure,
The most fragrant of roses,
Flower giver of life
So wonderfully delicate.

14

Nuestra Señora de Guadalupe *(Our Lady of Guadalupe). Bas relief polychromed retablo with leather and human hair, by Ray John de Aragón.*

✝ 24 ✝

BUENOS DÍAS PALOMA BLANCA
GOOD MORNING, O WHITE DOVE

This alabado is extremely popular and can be found in a multitude of variations in the copybooks of the Brothers. One version alludes to Our Lady of Guadalupe and her miraculous appearances before the Indian Juan Diego in Mexico in 1531. The following transcribed and translated version, however, is especially noteworthy in that, in stanza 5, there is a reference to mariners traveling at sea. The word *marinero* (mariner) refers to anyone traveling at sea, not just sailors. Since the Spanish for several centuries traveled by ship between Spain and the New World, it is likely that this alabado was sung during their journeys at sea.

Buenos días Paloma Blanca	Good Morning, O White Dove,
hoy te vengo a saludar	Today I come to salute you,
saludando tu belleza	Saluting your beauty
en tu reino celestial.	In your heavenly kingdom.
1	1
Eres madre del criador	You're the mother of the creator
que a mi corazón encanta	Who enchants so my heart,
gracias te doy con amor	Thanks I give you with much love,
buenos días Paloma Blanca.	Good morning, O White Dove.
2	2
Niña linda niña santa	Lovely child, holy child,
tu dulce nombre alabado	Your sweet name is so much praised,
porque eres tan sacrosanta	Because you are so sacred
yo te vengo a saludar.	I come today to greet you.
3	3

Reluciente como el alba
pura limpia y sin mancha
que gusto recibe mi alma
buenos días Paloma Blanca.

4

Feliz guía al marinero
eres la estrella del mar
en la tierra y en el cielo
yo te vengo a saludar.

5

Santísima Señora
en ti tengo mi esperanza
bella reluciente aurora
buenos días Paloma Blanca.

6

Pues que fuiste consebida
sin la culpa original
desde tu primer instante
en tu reino celestial.

7

Virgen celestial princesa
Virgen sagrada María
yo te alabo en este día
saludando tu belleza.

8

A ti graciosa niñita
hermosa perla oriental
que todo el orbe
ilumina
en tu reino celestial.

9

You sparkle like the dawn,
Pure in spirit without sin,
Oh what joy my soul receives,
Good morning, O white Dove.

4

Happy guide of the mariner,
You're the star of the sea
On the earth and in the heavens,
I come today to greet you.

5

O most holy, holy lady,
In you I have my hope,
Beautiful sparkling dawn,
Good morning, O White Dove.

6

You were conceived
Without original sin,
Since your genesis occurred
In your heavenly kingdom.

7

Celestial virgin and princess,
Sacred Virgin Mary,
I come today to praise you,
Saluting you on your beauty.

8

To you, O gracious child
Beautiful oriental pearl,
Whom the whole world makes
glowing
In your heavenly kingdom.

9

Echa con grande primor
de Dios la suma grandeza
porque nos ensartas en tu amor
saludando tu belleza.

10

Líbranos de todo mal
yo te pido gran señora
tú serás mi protectora
en tu reino celestial.

11

En la tierra y en el cielo
cantemos dulce alabanza
repitiendo con anhelo
buenos días Paloma Blanca.

12

Por ti no viene amargura
en este mísero suelo
siempre acudes Virgen pura
desde el azulado cielo.

13

Los ángeles en el cielo
Madre de Dios sacrosanta
todos por siempre te digan
buenos días Paloma Blanca.

14

You were made with so much skill,
God's most splendid creation,
Because you wrap us in your love,
We salute your beauty.

10

Liberate us from all sin,
I ask of you, O great lady,
You will be my own protector
In your heavenly kingdom.

11

On the earth and in the heavens,
We will sing your holy praises,
Repeating eagerly,
Good morning, O White Dove.

12

Through you there's nothing bitter
In this place of misery,
Virgin pure, you come to our calling
From the blueness of the sky.

13

The angels in the heavens,
O most Holy Mother of God,
Forever and ever they'll say,
Good morning, O White Dove.

14

Instrumentos de la Crucifixión *(Instruments of the Crucifixion). Nineteenth-century engraving. De Aragón family collection.*

Epilogue

In *la tierra encantada*, the land of enchantment, along the lush green banks of the Rio Grande, *la gente*, the people, lived, prayed, cried, and laughed. Spirits of the old ones nurtured the rich perfumed earth. Los Hispanos, the descendants of the Spanish colonists who arrived in the sixteenth century, understood the joyous meaning of life in the beautiful winding valleys, but they also felt the very forceful presence of Doña Sebastiana, Death.

The knowledge of being and passing was learned from *Los Antepasados*, those who came before. Their wonderful heritage was passed down through *los dichos* (sayings), like *Sal de la casa, y cuenta lo que te pasa* (Leave your home, and you will return telling of what happened to you) and *Dígame con quién andas y yo te diré quién eres* (Tell me who you are with and I will tell you who you are). *La morada de mi corazón* (the place where my heart is) touched the soul of the land, with references to the faith, the love, and the hopes of the people. Los dichos, mingling harmoniously with the haunting alabado chants of the Penitentes and *los cuentos de los ancianos*, the stories of the elders, flowed onward incessantly like the cool crisp waters of the river.

The Rio Grande here holds centuries of memories of the circle of life. The tears of happiness and of sorrow merge with the cleansing and life-giving rain to feed this enduring river and sometimes even slightly alter its course. The Indians first bathed in its purifying waters. They tasted the sweet fruits of God's marvelous creation as they hunted, gathered, and made their homes along the shores of the mighty *rio*. My people came after, sent by the king of Spain to settle in this frontier region of *La Nueva España*.

My ancestors arrived and lived with the land. They built their homes and places of worship out of the rich soil and crafted furnishings with their hands. Los Hispanos tilled the earth and planted the fields with the corn, beans, and pungent chiles that were among the gifts of their new homeland. They raised the cattle, sheep, and swine they brought over from Europe.

In my family, as in other Hispano families, the Spanish culture and traditions were preserved and maintained primarily by the female members. The men assisted, of course, but the home was a beehive of activity and learning guided by the mothers.

My mother, Cleofas Sánchez de Aragón, was born in Peñasco Blanco, near Mora, in 1915. There were twelve in her family, six boys and six girls. Her mother, Pablita Romero, was an orphan whose parents had been killed by the Indians. Life was hard on their farm but wonderful. The boys helped their father tend the livestock and care for the crops. The girls helped their mother gather plants in the hills for *remedios* (medicines) and to make their own brooms. They also gathered the roots of the amole yucca plant to make shampoo to wash their hair. They made soap, candles, cheese, butter—almost everything. What they didn't grow, raise, or make themselves they traded for at the yearly *mercado* (market), an open area on the plains where wagons from different villages gathered. Here my family traded beans, corn, peas, and chile for sugar and salt. They preserved fruits for the winter and made jellies and *carne seca* (beef jerky). Everyone worked from sunup until sundown, but they were happy. The girls in the family spread sheep blood on the hard-packed dirt floors of their home to make them harder, and the whole family sang songs and told *cuentos* (stories).

The cuentos were mainly about *La Llorona,* a frightening spirit who in life had killed her children and now returned in search of *malcreados* (disobedient children) to take with her. Stories about *El Coludo* (the long-tailed one, that is, the devil) were also popular, as were stories about *las brujas* (witches), the Indians, and *cosas extrañas* (strange things). All of these stories taught something, usually the importance of having respect and love for one another and a wholesome fear of the unknown. The message of the dichos was often basically the same: *¡Ayuda a otros y Dios te ayudara!* (Help others and God will help you!) This was what the Penitent Hermanos were all about.

Everyone helped everyone else. When someone died, the men built the coffin out of lumber they fashioned from the nearby trees in the woods, and the women draped it with *sabanilla* (cloth) and decorated it. The women tenderly bathed the body and carefully dressed it. The *velorio* (wake) was held at the home of the deceased, and the community followed the Hermanos in singing *canticos* (chants to prepare the soul for paradise), reciting rosaries, and mourning. Everyone dressed in black. A group of women mourners with black shawls, called *Las Dolientes,* attended every funeral as a group and sometimes sat off to one side, wailing

El Espiritú de la Tierra *(Spirit of the Land). Acrylic painting, by Ray John de Aragón. Courtesy Victor Grant Collection.*

the loudest. At the time of the funeral, the body would be wrapped in a white sheet from head to foot and replaced in the coffin and carried to the *camposanto* (the holy place, that is, the cemetery). The Penitentes and their families stopped at designated places called *descansos* (resting places), where everyone prayed and set small crosses in a pile of rocks in loving memory of the deceased.

The main influence on the collective psyche of the Penitente Brotherhood and on its organization, hymns, terminology, and Passion rituals was European, especially Spanish, and Christianity. The Penitentes put into practice the words of Pope St. Leo I (440–461), who placed great emphasis on the observance of the Passion:

> Our Lord's Passion is being continually reenacted until the end of the world; for just as, in the person of His saints, it is Christ Himself who is honored, it is Christ Himself who is loved; just as in the person of His poor, it is Christ Himself who is fed and clothed, so, in the person of all who suffer wrongs for justice' sake, it is Christ Himself who suffers.

The monastic orders and the monastic saints, including St. Bernard of Clairvaux and other itinerant barefoot preachers and hermits such as Joachim of Flora (circa 1130–1202) exerted a strong influence on the development of Penitente traditions, including cultivation of family and community spirit and the use of penitential practices. Unfortunately, the Penitentes would eventually be judged for their practices, not for their good deeds. Their loyalty to church doctrine was never questioned, but their method of expressing their faith was strongly criticized, and they were, like their predecessors, at times severely persecuted.

To an extent, religious and political unity had arisen in Spain in spite of the Moslem invasion. Rallying points were established by the Spanish Christians, and El Cid, Rúy (Rodrigo) Díaz de Bivar (1043 1099), emerged as a national hero. A Castillian knight, El Cid is regarded as the greatest figure of his age. He epitomized the pious spirit of the Spanish as well as the Christian ideal of family, church, and sovereign. With the fall of Granada in Spain, the final expulsion of the Moors, the conversion of Jews by St. Vincent Ferrer, and the discovery of America, a Spanish Christian spirit developed that would soon make itself felt around the world.

Queen Isabella of Castile and King Ferdinand of Aragón exercised considerable influence on the Christian conversion of the Americas. The Spanish queen held sway in questions of the faith, and she wielded power of a degree unmatched in the history of the world. Her own Castillian dialect was adopted as the national language, and Castillian thought became the Spanish norm. Queen Isabella made many honorable attempts at seeing that Christian ideals and principles were upheld in Spain's distant colonies. Christianity throughout Europe, including Spain, was kept in a condition of almost uninterrupted turmoil from the thirteenth to the fifteenth century as a result of the Black Death and warring factions within church and state.

Through the influence of Spanish friars and the Spanish Franciscan Pope, Christopher Columbus obtained a commission from the Spanish monarchs to make a voyage of exploration. This led, of course, to the discovery of the New World by Columbus in 1492, and to the conquest of Mexico by Hernán Cortés in 1521 and the entry of Franciscan friars into New Mexico by the late sixteenth century. Due to the isolation of New Mexico from civil and ecclesiastical seats of government in Mexico, flagellation was still practiced by both the Franciscan clergy and laymen up to and during the nineteenth century.

As the Franciscan clergy in New Mexico dwindled in number after Mexico's independence from Spain in 1821, the Third Order members, who began to be known as Penitentes, took a leading role in serving the spiritual needs of the people. However, after the rejection of Mexican secular priests stationed in New Mexico by the remaining Franciscans and New Mexicans, penitential practices became more exaggerated. New Mexicans had become accustomed to the brown habit of the Franciscans, and the religion of St. Francis was the only one they knew. Therefore, native-born secular priests, including Padre Martínez, basically followed Franciscan teachings and practices, as indicated by the appointment of Padre Martínez as Delegate Minister of the Third Order of St. Francis in 1826 by the last Franciscan Superior in New Mexico even though there were still nine Franciscans left in the territory.

It is not known exactly how much influence Padre Martínez exerted on the Penitentes. Nonetheless, his was the most enlightened and progressive mind of his age, and his overwhelming dedication to human rights and boundless compassion for the poor and the oppressed most certainly set an important example.

Friction between the Mexican-born clergy and the native priests and Hispanos developed as a result of the misunderstanding of local customs by the Mexicans. The strongly religious people of New Mexico had to carry out many of the religious functions themselves due to the scarcity of priests, and the Penitentes and the Carmelitas actually aided the clergy in the preservation of the Catholic faith. They lived under a very strict set of rules and did not tolerate improper or immoral behavior. Members of the Brotherhood were expected to serve as examples of decent comportment and virtue in the community or else face immediate expulsion.

With the entry of Americans into New Mexico, the traditional religious practices of the Spanish-speaking residents became endangered. The challenge to their culture made many New Mexicans seek spiritual comfort through self-mortification. Self-discipline, according to Christian tradition, increases at times of suffering, whether caused by illness, war, or confrontation with perceived heresy.

Besides performing penitential rites, the Penitente Brothers created impassioned works of art and composed heartrending religious hymns. Although derived from European antecedents, the locally produced art and poetry demonstrated the high degree of skill and the innovativeness of its makers.

In summary, the Penitentes and Carmelitas of New Mexico were able to unite the religious beliefs and rituals of the Old World with the culture of the Hispanos isolated in the remote mountains of New Mexico. Their influence as keepers of the Catholic faith and preservers of local customs has been far reaching, and many New Mexicans owe them a tremendous, if often unrecognized, debt.

My grandfather, Don Filimón Sánchez, and my mother's older brothers were members of the Brotherhood, and when the Lenten season came around, they took an active part in the Penitente rituals. My grandmother was a Carmelita. I

Penitente Paraphernalia. De Aragón family collection.

will never forget the vivid stories about Holy Week that my mother told me. The Lenten season was actually a little sad for my mother, since she did not get to see her father, brothers, and other male relatives for forty days. My mother would say goodbye to them and then would stand watching their procession until it disappeared over the rise.

During the following days, the girls did household chores while the other brothers chopped wood or did other jobs. Sometimes my grandmother visited with her *comadres* (friends). Things went on pretty much as before, but every day they were able to hear the alabados my grandfather and the other Penitentes sang echoing down through the valley late into the night. This aroused their curiosity, as did catching an occasional glimpse of the Brothers in procession from a distance. Finally Good Friday arrived, the day everyone gathered at the morada for the Passion Play and Tinieblas. It was a very vivid yet touching experience. At the end of the play, everyone was led into the morada, where candles were lit. The door was closed, and Tinieblas would begin.

On cue with the singing of an alabado, the candles were put out one by one until all were extinguished. In pitch darkness would be heard moans and groans, faint at first, then increasingly loud. By whirling matracas, rattling chains, beating on metal washtubs, and scraping on metal washboards, the Brothers created a cacophony of frightening sounds. "*Entre esto, los Penitentes se azotaban con las disciplinas* [during all of this, the Penitentes scourged their backs with the whips]," she would say. It seemed an eternity until the clamoring slowly stopped and the candles were relit, bringing the ritual to a conclusion. Then everyone left the morada and returned to their homes. The following day was full of joy as my grandfather and other relatives went back and their daily life slowly reverted to normal.

I will never forget the sad penitente chants that were sung at my grandfather's, grandmother's, and uncles' funerals. Nor will I forget visiting the chapels filled with the wooden santos and retablos of our people. I heard La Llorona wailing in the Arroyo Manteca behind my home. My memory happily lingers on thoughts of my uncle Juan García proudly saying he was a Penitente and that all of the Hermanos had designated duties, including the making of matracas, disciplinas, and santos. He made disciplinas, and he taught me how to weave the fibers from the amole plant to fashion them. I am also thankful that in growing up I was exposed to the wisdom contained in the dichos. My memories of all these things are steadily fading, however, and many of the customs and practices of the Penitentes have already disappeared irretrievably. This is truly unfortunate, in my view, since I strongly believe pride in the cultural heritage of New Mexico will help us forge ahead into the future. Los Hermanos de la Luz stood for faith, family, community, and cultural pride. Hopefully this book will help make their nobility of mind and spirit and their idealistic efforts at maintaining profound religious faith and a sense of community in the face of vast social changes more widely known and more greatly appreciated.

APPENDIX:

Spanish Medieval Christian Poetry

The following examples of the Medieval Christian lyric poetry of Spain reflect characteristics of composition and structure similar to those found in alabados of New Mexico. This strongly supports a clear genealogy of Christian poetic expression from the Spanish Old World to the Spanish New World of New Mexico.

Fray Yñigo de Mendoza from *Fabla la Verónica*:

¿Dónde vas apasyonado	Where do you go so much affected
con tan diuersas feridas,	With such diverse wounds,
con espinas coronado,	With thorns so coronated,
con color descolorado,	With your color discolorated,
con lágrimas tan sentidas,	With tears so much felt,
con gentes desconoscidas,	With people who were strangers,
con falsas acusaciones?	With false accusations?
¿Tus gracias jamás oydas,	Your graces no longer heard,
por ventura son perdidas,	Through casualty they're lost,
que vas entre dos ladrones?	That you go between two thieves?

Fray Yñigo de Mendoza from *Por Sant Juan lo Dize*:

Vna corona de espinas,
vna coluna pesada,
vnas fuertes disciplinas,
vnas marlotas sanguinas,
vna soga ensangrentada,
vna cruz mal cepillada,
clauos, martillo, escallera,
vna fiel auinagrada,
cana y lança enazerada
son tus armas y vandera.

A crown of thorns,
A heavy column,
Some strong whips,
Some sanguine robes,
A bloodied rope,
A cross that is badly planed,
Nails, hammer, ladder,
A vinegary sponge,
A pole and shafted lance
Are your arms and banner.

Juan Alvarez Gato from *Al Crucificio*:

Adórote, Santa Cruz,
aruol dulce de verdad,
do alunbró la ceg/u/edad
nestra verdadera luz,
do el Señor de los señores
que con tres clauos sostienes,
dando fin a sus dolores,
dio comienáço a nuestros bienes.

We adore you holy cross,
Sweet tree of truth,
You illumine the darkness
You are our true light,
Where the lord of the lords
With three nails you suspended,
Bringing to an end his pains,
And where all our benefits started.

Juan de Padilla from *Retablo de la vida de Cristo*:

Yo Poncio Pilato, juez ordenado
por el romano monarca sereno,
mando que muera Jesús
Nazareno
ásperamente en la cruz enclavado;
y mando, que súbitamente soltado
sea el ladrón que pedís y queréis;

I, Pontius Pilate, judge ordained
By the serene Roman monarch,
Do command that
Jesus die
Rudely nailed on the cross;
I command that quickly be released
That thief you want and so desire;

pero vosotros en fin lo veréis,	But all of you in the end will see,
veréis el efecto de aqueste pecado	You will see the effect of this sin.
La cruz allegada, los muy condenados,	The cited cross, those much condemned,
probados jueces, ministros malignos,	The tested judges, malicious ministers,
ponerla mandaron a los hornecinos	To place it ordered all the degenerate ones
sobre los hombros de Cristo sagrados.	On the sacred shoulders of Christ.
Ya los pregoneros, muy bien acordados,	The town criers, so well reminded,
le pregonaban con altos pregones;	Announced his conviction with loud shouts;
sonaban las trompas los grandes poltrones,	The trumpets blared out the sounds of the wretched,
que suenan delante los sentenciados	That sound before the ones so condemned.
Cayó con la cruz mi Señor delicado,	He fell with the cross, my delicate Lord,
porque sus fuerzas aquí desmayabanç	Because his strength had worn down,
palos y lozes, y priesa le daban,	A beating with sticks, kicks, and shovings they gave him,
a causa que fuese muy más quebrantado.	All of which caused him to break further down.
Y toman los malos un hombre llamado	And the bad ones take a man called
Simon Cirineo, que presto llevase	Simon the Cyrenaic, who quickly took on

la Cruz dolorida, por bien que pesase,	The painful cross, which was so heavy,
hasta el Calvario, lugar diputado.	Up to Calvary, the designated place.

Yñigo López de Mendoza, Marques de Santillana, from *Invocación a Dios*:

Con manífica paçiençia	With magnificent patience
esperas al pecador,	You wait for the sinner,
llamándole a penitença	Calling him to do penance
con ynçesable clamor;	With unceasing cries;
al penitente converso	The penitent convert
reçibes a piedad;	In piety you receive;
dañas con seneridad	You punish with swiftness
al obstinado peruerso.	Those obstinate and perverse.

Anonymous from *Cánticos del via-crucis:*

Poderoso Jesús Nazareno,	All powerful Jesus of Nazareth,
de los cielos y tierra Rey universal,	Of the heavens and earth universal king,
hoy un alma que os tiene ofendido	Today a soul that has so offended you
pide que sus culpas queráis perdonar.	Asks that his faults you will forgive.
Viernes Santo, qué dolor,	Good Friday, oh what pain,
expiró crucificado	Died crucified
Cristo, nuestro Redentor,	Christ, our Redeemer,
mas antes dijo, angustiado,	Said, anguished,
siete palabras de amor.	Seven words of love.

Anonymous from *Cántico contemplativo de la Pasión* (1584):

En la alta vera cruz	On the high true cross
está pediente el cordero	The gentle man is hanging
nuestro Dios y redemptor	Our God and our redeemer
nuestro bien nuestro consuelo	Our goodness our consolation
su sancto cuerpo precioso	His precious holy body
de sangre todo cubierto	All covered with his blood
el su Diuino costado	His divine side
con la lança lo tiene abierto	With lance has been pierced
el cuerpo descoyuntado	His body all disjointed
enclauado en el madero	Nailed on the timber
en la su lacra cabeca	On his wounded head
corona de la corona	Crown of all crowns
pássanle todo el celebro	Passes through his brain
por el pecado de Adán	For the sin of Adam
el nuestro padre primero	Who was our first father
todo lo sufre por mí	He suffered all for me
por librarnos del infierno	To liberate us from the inferno
a su padre está rogando	To his father he is pleading
por los que allí lo pusieron	For those who placed him there
perdónalos dixo padre	Forgive them our father asks
que no saben qué se hizieron	For they know not what they do
al pie de la santa cruz	At the foot of the holy cross
está su madre gimiendo	His mother is lamenting
junto a ella está sant Iuan	Next to her is good Saint John
entristecido plañendo	Sadly in bewailment
y también la Magdalena	And also the Magdalene
muchas lágrimas vertiendo	Many tears she is shedding
vezina le es ya la muerte	Neighbor, death is near

a nuestro Dio verdadero	To our one true God
morir quiere humanidad	Dying is his humanity
diuino queda biuiendo	Divine he will be living
jamas esto feneció	Forever to conclude
en nuestro Dios trino vero	In our God the trinity
boluió su rostro a la madre	He turned his head to see his mother
con muy afligido aspecto	Who was so much afflicted
encomendóla a sant Iuan	And commended her to Saint John
estas palabras diziendo	With these words saying
muger cata ay tu hijo	Woman behold there your son
y a ti por madre la entrego	And you as mother I convey
gran pasión tomó la virgen	In great anguish the Virgin was
en ver morir su consuelo	On the death of her dear joy
llegó la ora de sexta	The hour of the sixth arrived
ya la muerte viene cedo	Death arrives immediately
con boz alta temerosa	With tremorous high voice
lo que dixo, yo refiero	What he said, I now refer
padre mio en las tus manos	My father into your hands
el mi espíritu encomiendo	I my spirit do commend
salida que fue su alma	His soul thus left
del sancto Diuino cuerpo	His holy body so divine
la tierra toda temblo	The earth thus trembled
toda se cubrio de duelo	And was covered all in gloom
el velo por medio se rompe	The veil ripped in two
que estava dentro en el templo	Deep within the temple
las aues las animalias	The animals and birds
todas hazen sentimiento	All shared the sorrowful grief
en ver morir a mi Dios	On seeing my God die
siente allas lo que siento.	They regret what I regret.

Bibliography

Ahlborn, Richard E. *The Penitente Moradas of Abiquiu*. Washington, D.C.: Smithsonian Institution Press, 1968.

Alonso, Martín. *Enciclopedia del Idioma*. Madrid: Aguilar, S.A. de Ediciones, 1958.

American Bible Society. *The Good News Bible*. New York: American Bible Society, 1978.

Aribau, D., and Carlos Buenaventura. *Biblioteca de Autores Españoles*. Madrid: Real Academia Española, 1944.

Attwater, Donald, comp. *A Dictionary of Saints*. New York: P. J. Kennedy and Sons, 1958.

Austin, Mary. *The Land of Journey's Ending*. New York: The Century Co., 1924.

Beatty and Johnson, eds. *Heritage of Western Civilization*. Englewood Cliffs, N. J.: Prentice Hall, 1966.

Berceo, Gonzalo de. *Veintitres milagros: nuevo manuscrito de la Real Academia Española*. Impr. de Libreria y casa editorial Hernando, S.A., 1929.

___. *Milagros de Nuestra Señora*. Espasa-Calpe, S.A., 1934.

Boerger, Berard. "Reflecting on St. Francis' Devotion to Mary." *Our Sunday Visitor,* October 4, 1987.

Boyd, E. *Popular Arts of Spanish New Mexico*. Santa Fe: Museum of New Mexico Press, 1974.

Broderick, Robert C. *The Catholic Encyclopedia*. New York: Thomas Nelson Inc., 1975.

Brown, Lorin W. *Hispano Folklife of New Mexico*. Albuquerque: University of New Mexico Press, 1978.

Bullock, Alice. *Living Legends of Santa Fe Country*. Santa Fe, N.M.: Ancient City Press, 1972.

Burke, James T. *This Miserable Kingdom*. Las Vegas, N.M.: Our Lady of Sorrows Church, 1973.

Carroll, H. Bailey, and J. Villasana Haggard. *Three New Mexico Chronicles*. Albuquerque, N.M.: Quivira Society, 1942.

Cejados, D. Julio y Frauca. *Vocabulario Medieval Castellano*. New York: Las Américas Publishing Co., 1968.

Chávez, Tibo J. *New Mexican Folklore of the Rio Abajo*. Portales, N.M.: Bishop Printing Co., 1972.

Córdova, Lorenzo de. *Echoes of the Flute*. Santa Fe, N.M.: Ancient City Press, 1985.

Courtney, F. J. *New Catholic Encyclopedia.* New York: McGraw-Hill, 1967.

Crandall, Robert W., ed. *Encyclopedia of World Art*. New York: McGraw-Hill, 1958.

Cruz, Joan Carroll. *Relics*. Huntington, Ind.: Our Sunday Visitor, Inc., 1984.

Cuyler, L. E. *New Catholic Encyclopedia.* New York: McGraw-Hill, 1967.

Darley, Alex M. *The Passionists of the Southwest*. Glorieta, N.M.: Rio Grande Press, 1968.

de Aragón, Ray John. "El Padre Martínez y el Obispo Lamy." *La Luz Magazine*, April 1972.

___. "El Conciliador: Resumen de la Vida del Padre Antonio José Martínez." *El Hispano*, July 1975.

___. "Vida del Padre Antonio José Martínez." *El Hispano*, July 1975.

___. *Padre Martínez and Bishop Lamy*. Las Vegas, N.M.: Pan-American Publishing Co., 1976.

___. "El Santero de Mora." *El Hispano*, June 1978.

___. "Mora Intrigue and Murder." *New Mexico Magazine*, August 1982.

___. "Padre Martínez Memory Scarred." *Taos News*, August 1983.

___. *Padre Martínez: New Perspectives from Taos*. Taos, N.M.: Millicent Rogers Museum, 1988.

DeBorhegyi, Stephen F. *El Santuario de Chimayó*. Santa Fe, N.M.: The Spanish Colonial Arts Society, 1956.

de Hita, Arcipreste. *Libro de Buen Amor.* Mexico: Editorial. Porrua, S.A., 1980.

de la Vega, Roberto. *The Three Centuries of Tomé, New Mexico*. Los Lunas, N.M.: Saint Clement Church, 1976.

de Venette, Jean. *The Chronicle.* Translated by Richard Newhall. New York: Columbia University Press, 1953.

Díaz-Plaja, D. Guillermo. *Historia General de las Literaturas Hispanicas*. Barcelona: Editorial Vergara, 1969.

Edman, V. Raymond. *The Light in Dark Ages*. Wheaton, Ill.: Van Kamper Press, 1949.

Eliade, Mircea, ed. *The Encyclopedia of Religion*. New York: Macmillan, 1987.

Espinosa, Aurelio M. *The Folklore of Spain in the American Southwest*. Norman: University of Oklahoma Press, 1985.

Farrow, John. *Pageant of the Popes*. St. Paul, Minn.: Catechetical Guild Educational Society, 1955.

Fleming, William. *Art, Music and Ideas*. New York: Holt, Rinehart and Winston, 1970.

Fouard, Abbé Constant. *Christ the Son of God*. London: Longmans, Green and Co., 1890.

Froissart, Jean. *Chronicles.* Translated by Geoffrey Bereton. Baltimore: Penguin, 1968.

Garciano, Carmelo. *Análisis Estilístico de los "Milagros de Nuestra Señora" de Berceo*. Madrid: Editorial Gredos, 1971.

Gierke, Otto. *Political Theories of the Middle Ages*. Boston:

Beacon Press, 1958.
Gombrich, E. H. *The Story of Art*. New York: Phaidon, 1968.
Gooch, Brison D., ed. *Interpreting Western Civilization*. Homewood, Ill.: Dorsey Press, 1969.
Gottfried, Robert S. *The Black Death*. New York: Macmillan, 1983.
Hacker, John G. *Catholic Hymnal*. New York: William H. Sadlier, Inc., 1920.
Hadas, Moses. *A History of Rome*. New York: Doubleday, 1956.
Hamilton, Edith. *The Roman Way*. New York: W. W. Norton, 1960.
Henderson, Alice Corbin. *Brothers of Light*. New York: Harcourt Brace, 1937.
Hilpisch, Stephanus. *Benedictinism through the Changing Centuries*. Collegeville, Minn.: St. John's Abbey Press, 1958.
Hoever, Hugo. *Lives of the Saints*. New York: Catholic Book Publishing Co., 1977.
Horgan, Paul. *Lamy of Santa Fe*. New York: Farrar, Straus, and Giroux, 1975.
Horton, Rod W., and Vincent F. Hopper. *Background of European Literature*. New York: Appleton-Century-Crofts, 1954.
Hughes, Dom Anselm, ed. *Early Medieval Music up to 1300*. New York: Oxford University Press, 1976.
Hughes, Philip. *A Popular History of the Catholic Church*. Garden City, N.Y.: Doubleday, 1960.
Isla, Amancio Bolaño E. *Arcipreste de Hita*. Mexico: Editorial Purrua, 1980.
___. *Gonzalo de Berceo*. Mexico: Editorial Purrua, 1981.
Jenkins, Myra Ellen, and Albert H. Schroeden. *A Brief History of New Mexico*. Albuquerque: University of New Mexico Press, 1974.
Keller, John Esten. *Gonzalo de Berceo*. New York: Twayne Publishers, 1972.
Kieckhefer, Richard. *Dictionary of the Middle Ages*. New York: Scribner's, 1982.

Little, A. G. "The Mendicant Orders." In *Cambridge Medieval History,* edited by J. R. Tanner, C. W. Previté-Orton, and Z. N. Brooke." 9 vols. New York: Macmillan, 1911.

Lippy, Charles H., and Peter W. Williams. *Encyclopedia of the American Religious Experience*. New York: Scribner's, 1988.

Machlis, Joseph. *The Enjoyment of Music*. New York: W. W. Norton, 1957.

Magill, Frank N., ed. *Great Lives from History*. Pasadena, Calif.: History Salem Press, 1989.

Marie, Sister Joseph. *The Role of the Church and the Folk in the Development of the Early Drama in New Mexico*. Philadelphia: University of Pennsylvania Press, 1948.

Mather, Christine. *Colonial Frontiers*. Santa Fe, N.M.: Ancient City Press, 1983.

McCoy, Robert B. *The Catholic Encyclopedia.* New York: Thomás Nelson, Inc., Publishers, 1975.

McDonald, William J., ed. *New Catholic Encyclopedia*. New York: McGraw-Hill, 1967.

McSorley, Joseph. *An Outline History of the Church by Centuries*. St. Louis: Herder Book Co., 1945.

Mead, Margaret, ed. *Cultural Patterns and Technical Change*. New York: New American Library of World Literature, 1961.

Miller, Hugh M. *History of Music*. New York: Barnes & Noble, 1968.

Moliner, María. *Diccionario de Uso del Español*. Madrid: Editorial Gredos, 1966.

Moulton, Richard G. *The Literary Study of the Bible*. New York: D. C. Heath, 1899.

Murray, Desmond. *A Saint of the Week*. St. Paul, Minn.: Catechetical Guild Educational Society, 1955.

Painter, Sidney. *A History of the Middle Ages*. New York: Knopf, 1956.

Panofsky, Erwin. *Studies in Iconology*. New York: Harper and Row, 1972.

The Poem of The Cid. Translated by Lesley Byrd Simpson. Berkeley: University of California Press, 1957.

Poupard, Dennis, ed. *Literature Criticism from 1400 to 1800*. Detroit: Gale Research Co., 1984.

Proske, Beatrice Gilman. *Juan Martínez Montañés, Sevillian Sculptor*. New York: Hispanic Society of America, 1967.

Robb, John Donald. *Hispanic Folk Songs of New Mexico*. Albuquerque: University of New Mexico Press, 1954.

Robles, Federico Carlos Sainz de. *Diccionario de la literatura*. Madrid: Aguilar, 1965.

Roth, Cecil, ed. *Encyclopedia Judaica*. New York: Macmillan, 1972.

Sánchez, Pedro. *Memorias Sobre La Vida del Presbitero Don Antonio José Martínez*. Translated by Ray John de Aragón. Santa Fe, N.M.: The Lightening Tree, 1978.

Santamaría, Francisco J. *Diccionario General de Americanismos*. Mexico: Editorial Pedro Robredo, 1942.

Shalkop, Robert L. *Reflections of Spain*. Colorado Springs, Colo.: Taylor Museum, 1968.

Simpson, D. P. *Cassell's Latin Dictionary*. New York: Macmillan, 1968.

Stanley, F. *The Tomé, New Mexico, Story,* Tex.: F. Stanley, 1966.

Steele, Thomas J. *Holy Week in Tomé*. Santa Fe, N.M.: Sunstone Press, 1976.

___. *Santos and Saints*. Santa Fe, N.M.: Ancient City Press, 1982.

___. *Penitente Self-Government*. Santa Fe, N.M.: Ancient City Press, 1985.

Strayer, Joseph R., ed. *Dictionary of the Middle Ages*. New York: Scribner's, 1982.

Tate, Bill. *The Penitentes of the Sangre de Cristos*. Truchas, N.M.: Tate Gallery, 1968.

Toor, Frances. *A Treasury of Mexican Folkways*. New York: Crown, 1947.

Toynbee, Arnold J. *A Study of History*. New York: Dell, 1965.
Verostko, R. J. *The Encyclopedia of Religion.*
Weigle, Marta. *Brothers of Light, Brothers of Blood*. Albuquerque: University of New Mexico Press, 1976.
Weigle, Marta, ed. *Hispanic Arts and Ethnohistory in the Southwest*. Santa Fe, N.M.: Ancient City Press, 1983.
White, Aurora Lucero. *Los Hispanos*. Denver: Sage Books, 1947.
Willey, Basil. *The Seventeenth Century Background: The Thought of the Age in Relation to Religion and Poetry*. Garden City, N.Y.: Doubleday, 1935.
Woody, Kennerly M. *Dictionary of the Middle Ages.* New York: Scribner's, 1982.
Wroth, William. *Christian Images in Hispanic New Mexico*. Colorado Springs, Colo.: Taylor Museum, 1982.
Zinsser, Hans. *Rats, Lice and History*. New York: Bantam, 1965.

Notes

1. Lorin W. Brown, *Hispano Folklife of New Mexico* (Albuquerque: University of New Mexico Press, 1978), 184.
2. The Passion is the suffering, both interior and exterior, endured by Jesus Christ from the Last Supper until his death on the cross. The earliest Latin use of the term *passio* refers to the entirety of the paschal mystery, and this includes the Resurrection and the Ascension as well as the sufferings of Good Friday.
3. Bill Tate, *The Penitentes of the Sangre de Cristos* (Truchas, N.M.: Tate Gallery, 1968), 8.
4. St. Ignatius, a disciple of St. John, maintained a special desire to suffer with Christ. In A.D. 107 St. Ignatius was martyred.
5. Rom. 4:9.
6. E. W. McDonnell, *New Catholic Encyclopedia* (New York: McGraw-Hill, 1967), vol. 1, 698.
7. Joseph McSorley, *An Outline History of the Church by Centuries* (St. Louis: B. Herder Book Co., 1945), 312.
8. Kennerly M. Woody, *Dictionary of the Middle Ages* (New York: Scribner's, 1982), 509.
9. Hugo Hoever, *Lives of the Saints* (New York: Catholic Book Publishing Co., 1977), 287–288.
10. Alex M. Darley, *The Passionists of the Southwest* (Glorieta, N.M.: Rio Grande Press, 1968), 73.
11. F. J. Courtney, *New Catholic Encyclopedia* (New York: McGraw-Hill, 1967), vol. 5, 954–55.

12. Berard Boerger, "Reflecting on St. Francis' Devotion to Mary," *Our Sunday Visitor*, October 4, 1987.
13. McSorley, *An Outline History of the Church by Centuries*, 400.
14. A. G. Little, "The Mendicant Orders," in *Cambridge Medieval History*, ed. J. R. Tanner, C. W. Previté-Orton, and Z. N. Brooke, 9 vols. (New York: Macmillan, 1911–1936), vol. 6, 755.
15. There are three stages in the history of flagellation in the Christian Church: (1) it was in use as a punishment from the fourth century on, (2) it developed as a form of voluntary penance in the middle of the eleventh century, and (3) it began to be employed as a feature of public penitential processions in the thirteenth century.
16. Jean de Venette, *The Chronicle,* trans. Richard Newhall (New York: Columbia University Press, 1953), 51–52.
17. Jean Froissart, *Chronicles*, trans. Geoffrey Bereton (Baltimore: Penguin, 1968), 111–12.
18. Richard Kieckhefer, *Dictionary of the Middle Ages* (New York: Scribner's, 1982), 77.
19. Darley, *Passionists of the Southwest*, 73–75.
20. Hoever, *Lives of the Saints*, 136.
21. Ibid., 313.
22. McSorley, *An Outline History of the Church by Centuries*, 568.
23. Ibid., 570.
24. Alice Corbin Henderson, *Brothers of Light* (New York: Harcourt, Brace, 1937), 63–64.
25. McSorley, *An Outline History of the Church by Centuries*, 646.
26. Henderson, *Brothers of Light*, 8–9.
27. James T. Burke, *This Miserable Kingdom* (Las Vegas, N.M.: Our Lady of Sorrows Church, 1973), 133–39.
28. Ibid., 141–42.
29. Ibid., 142–43.

30. Marta Weigle, *Brothers of Light, Brothers of Blood* (Albuquerque: University of New Mexico Press, 1976), 35, 197.
31. E. Boyd, *Popular Arts of Spanish New Mexico* (Santa Fe: Museum of New Mexico Press, 1974), 442.
32. Thomas J. Steele, *Holy Week in Tomé* (Santa Fe, N.M. Sunstone Press, 1976), 5.
33. Richard E. Ahlborn, *The Penitente Moradas of Abiquiu* (Washington, D.C.: Smithsonian Institution Press, 1968), 126.
34. The representation of *Nuestro Padre Jesús Nazareno* (Our Father Jesus the Nazarene) is of the scourged, thorn-crowned, purple-robed Jesus. The santo is usually a bulto, nearly life-size, hinged at the shoulders, and bearing the marks of the Passion. To the Penitentes, it stands for forgiveness or mortal sin; penitence; the daily cross; faith, hope, and charity; and a good death.
35. The statue of *Nuestra Señora de los Dolores* represents Mary enduring the sorrows predicted in Luke 2:35, especially the Crucifixion of Jesus. It shows Mary standing with her hands folded, being pierced through the heart by a sword or seven swords, and wearing a red gown and a cowl. There is a definite Penitente interest, since it is usually Nuestra Señora de los Dolores who engages in the Encuentro as Christ moves toward Calvary.
36. Weigle, *Brothers of Light, Brothers of Blood*, 44.
37. Boyd, *Popular Arts of Spanish New Mexico*, 443–44.
38. H. Bailey Carroll and J. Villasana Haggard, *Three New Mexico Chronicles* (Albuquerque, N.M.: Quivira Society, 1942), 236–37.
39. Weigle, *Brothers of Light, Brothers of Blood*, 45.
40. Ibid., 48.
41. Ibid., 45–46
42. F. Stanley, *The Tomé, New Mexico, Story* (Tex.: F. Stanley, 1966), 8.
43. Decree reprinted in Ray John de Aragón, *Padre Martínez and*

Bishop Lamy (Las Vegas, N.M.: Pan-American Publishing Co., 1976), 18–19.

44. Carroll and Haggard, *Three New Mexico Chronicles*, 53.
45. Paul Horgan, *Lamy of Santa Fe* (New York: Farrar, Straus, and Giroux, 1975), 407.
46. The Third Order, established in 1221 under the name The Brothers and Sisters of Penance, based their rule on that of the Franciscan Order. Although the Third Order of St. Francis is the best known and the largest, it is not the oldest. For example, the Carmelite Order dates its founding to 1154, when St. Berthold, a monk from Calabria, established a community of hermits on Mount Carmel. The Carmelites received approval of their rule in 1226.
47. Weigle, *Brothers of Light, Brothers of Blood*, 144; Marta Weigle, ed., *Hispanic Arts and Ethnohistory in the Southwest* (Santa Fe, N.M.: Ancient City Press, 1983), 33.
48. Edward Berry, interview by Ray John de Aragón, January 4, 1986, Tomé, New Mexico.
49. Jesusita Aragón, interview by Ray John de Aragón, November 8, 1985, Las Vegas, New Mexico.
50. Brown, *Hispano Folklife of New Mexico*, 113.
51. Thomas J. Steele, *Santos and Saints* (Santa Fe, N.M.: Ancient City Press, 1974, 175.
52. McSorley, *An Outline History of the Church by Centuries*, 58, 84, 117.; R. J. Verostko, *The Encyclopedia of Religion*, 45–54.; also, *The Catholic Encyclopedia*, 872–81.
53. *Death Hunting the Hunters*, series of woodcuts from Geiler Von Kaisersperg's sermons, *De arbore humana*, printed by Johann Gruninger, Strassburg, 1514.
54. Robert L. Shalkop, *Reflections of Spain* (Colorado Springs, Colo.: The Taylor Museum, 1968), 7.
55. Boyd, *Popular Arts of Spanish New Mexico*, 98–102.

56. During the era of the Black Death in Europe, plague victims were placed outside door entrances of buildings to be transported every morning in death carts to the burial holes.
57. Alice Corbin Henderson, who witnessed a Penitente procession in Abiquiu, New Mexico, in 1935, described the death cart as follows:

Following the cross-bearers came a penitent dragging the *Carreta del Muerto*. This was a very heavy low wooden cart, with solid wooden wheels, like the old ox-carts. On it sat a small figure of Death, clothed in a rusty black dress, with staring obsidian eyes in a chalk-white face. The eyes caught whatever glint of light fell upon them, even though the face was in shadow, giving to the dead mask an uncanny sense of life. The figure held a drawn bow with the arrow stretched for flight. Tradition has it that the arrow once left the bow to strike the heart of a mocking bystander, killing him instantly. Variations of this tradition exist through all the mountain villages and are occasionally applied to some specific person, long since dead.

Sometimes the figure on the cart is blindfolded, indicating death's blind uncertainty. Also other primitive instruments of death are sometimes concealed in the cart—an ax-head, a stone hammer, or a heavy rock.

The figure of death is in reality a carefully carved skeleton; and some of these figures are very finely conceived, with beautiful articulation of form.

The penitent dragged the *Carreta del Muerto* by a horse-hair rope passed over his shoulders and under his arm-pits, the painful rite of the dragging cart cutting into his naked flesh—a penance as severe as any other, and increased by the fact that the axles of the cart were stationary, and where there was a turn in the path, the entire cart and its inflexible wheels were dragged by main strength; (Henderson, *Brothers of Light*, 32–33).

58. The favorite images of the Penitentes included San Francisco de Asís, Santa Rita de Casia, and Santa Rosalía de Palermo, all saints that were shown holding a cross in one hand and contemplating a skull they held in the other.

59. Alonso Martín, *Enciclopedia del Idioma* (Madrid: Aquilar, S.A. de Ediciones, 1958), 198.
60. Ernest Hunter Wright and Mary Heritage Wright, eds., *Man's Earliest Music*, vol. 11 of *Richards Topical Encyclopedia* (New York: The Richards Company, 1951), 204–05.
61. Ibid., 211–12.
62. Monophonic music is music that consists of a single melodic line.
63. Joseph Machlis, *The Enjoyment of Music* (New York: W. W. Norton, 1957), 257–59.
64. At the end of the fifteenth century, Giovanni di Fidanza was canonized by the Franciscan Pope Sixtus IV. He was also credited with a series of ascetic poems. An ascetic is someone who renounces companionship and comfort and embraces self-mortification and religious devotion.
65. Arcipreste de Hita, *Libro de Buen Amor* (Mexico: Editorial Porrua, S.A., 1980), 237.
66. L. E. Cuyler, *New Catholic Encyclopedia*, vol. 13 (New York: McGraw-Hill, 1967), 625–26.

Alabados by Title

Spanish

English

Heartsfire Books